MW00337784

PATRIOTS BETRAYED

A Soldier, Scholar, Spy's Warning about America´s Leadership Crisis

David Baumblatt

TEREBINTH

PUBLISHING

Patriots Betrayed

Copyright © 2023 by David Baumblatt

Paperback ISBN: 978-1-956033-07-6

Hardcover ISBN: 978-1-956033-08-3

In honor of my father, Bruce Robert Baumblatt, who gave me the strength to stand alone in the darkness. His patriotic service to the country is a testament to all military veterans who have sacrificed their lives, so Americans can live free.

Left to right: Bruce Baum (father), David Baumblatt, Ruth Baum (mother), Jon Baum (brother) at Jon´s graduation from the Air Force Officer Training School in 2000 at Maxwell Air Force Base in Montgomery, Alabama. During his commissioning ceremony, I had the honor and privilege to administer the US Uniformed Services Oath of Office to him.

Where there is courage, there is no loneliness
Where there is loyalty, there is love

Contents

Acknowledgments

First, I would like to thank dear Brigadier General Walter Kastenmayer, your leadership principles of selfless service and mentorship have not been forgotten; you were a father figure to me. I will be forever thankful; may you continue to rest in peace. To General Kastenmayer's living family members: your family has earned an honorable legacy through the deeds of this great man. I and so many other MMI graduates are dearly grateful to him.

Dear Dennis "Denny" Slater, thank you for being my scout master; through your patriotism and selfless service you taught us young Boy Scouts of Troop 41, Roxbury, New York, the importance of helping your community through public service. It was through your help that I was able to achieve the Eagle Scout Award. Thank you so much Denny; I will never forget you.

I would also like to give my sincere thanks to the Chinese law firm that came to my aid from the illegal and unethical actions taken against me by the Boeing Company and defended me in my legal battle against this American Globalist Corporation. To the Kang Da Law Firm (康达律师事务所) ,[1] thank you so much; your professionalism and expertise was second to none. I highly recommend this law firm: http://en.kangdalawyers.com/. Specifically, to my lawyer XuShuo (许硕), thank you for defending the reputation of an American military veteran from the unpatriotic American military-industrial complex.[2]

Introduction

An American Patriot's battle with the Enemy of America

A West Point graduate and former FBI Special Agent who was assigned to work foreign counterintelligence with the mission to hunt down Foreign Spies in order to protect America, I now am being hunted by my very own government. I left the FBI back in 2007 due to the bureau's corrupt culture. Nothing has changed. Fully aware of America's decline, I decided to leave America back in 2010. During my last visit to America, I was detained, interrogated, searched, humiliated, surveilled, deceived, and assaulted by the American government. I have been designated an enemy of the state.

This attack on my honor has propelled me to take this fight to the American people through his book. The founder and CEO of Terebinth Leadership Advisory, I left the FBI back in 2007 due to his grievances with the bureau's corrupt culture, which he had personally witnessed and experienced; however, yet again, the US government is continuing its same immoral and illegal conduct by spying on not only him, but also on so many other innocent American citizens as well. Having already become fully aware of America's decline into a rapidly approaching collapse or civil war, I decided to leave America back in 2010.

The deterioration of American's individual freedoms and civil liberties can be attributed to the tyrannical corruption and collusion between the globalist American government and globalist American corporations. Having personally lived in China for over ten years, I have seen firsthand how these globalist American corporations continue to value China over America, how these globalist American corporations dismiss the American people and will sell their products and services on the global market to the highest bidder regardless of whether these economic transactions are in the best interest to the American people or not. Together these two entities—the American government and the American corporations—are working together to undermine the freedoms of the American people and the country itself. I have long since lost trust in the godless globalist American government and American corporations; and you should not trust them either.

This book is about the decline of patriotic leadership and the continued rise of liberal globalism that is dooming America. As trust in the American government continues to be eroded by this liberal globalist ideology, American citizens are slowly realizing that there will be no easy solution to their country's dilemma and that violence and chaos may in fact be what is in store for the country. In this book I provide leadership lessons and political insights based on my cumulative real-world experiences in life, work, and study. Despite my liberal indoctrination at Harvard, I am a staunch freedom-loving conservative who believes that the moral leadership of America is dying in the cavities of the liberal globalist abyss and that the political correctness of today's American media, government, and corporations will only continue to hide the fact that America is continuing down a path of decline that will sooner or later reach a breaking point. And as all great empires collapse so too will America. This is a warning to American patriots, a warning to prepare yourselves as the globalist American empire continues to destroy the once free and conservative America.

The biggest threat to the American people is not from the typically propagandized foreign actors, such as China, Russia, Iran, Islam, and North Korea. The real threat to the American people is from their very own big government and big corporations. These two American entities pose the greatest threat to the constitutional protections which have safeguarded the freedoms of the American people throughout history. As they continue to expand in size and power, their globalist agenda will continue to transform what was once a free conservative-capitalist America into a repressive liberal-socialist nation. The America today is not in line with what our revolutionary forefathers and founders of this great country had intended. Just as our American forefathers escaped the tyranny of England's repressive taxation and control, today's American government is replicating this same form of tyranny with ever-increasing authority over its citizens. As the government continues to oppress the American people, just as in the days of the revolution, the memories of 1776 will come back to haunt today's American government; the Sons of Liberty are assembling against the destructive political ideologies poisoning the nation today: multiculturalism, diversity, feminism, globalism, socialism, communism, open borders, atheism, materialism. All these liberal globalist ideologies are weaponized lies and perversion which have one goal in mind: To destroy the Conservative America which values *faith, family,* and *freedom.* Patriotic Americans are tired of these divisive dogmas being thrown at them from an unpatriotic government as well as unpatriotic corporations.

If you are an American Patriot who values your personal freedoms, then this book is a battle cry for you. Lacking any evidence against me, this unethical government investigation against me is due to the FBI's biased against my strong conservative political views. I have formally presented my grievances to the US government and have been ignored. This book is a warning to all Americans. If the constitutional rights and freedoms of a military veteran who has honorably served his country, can so easily be trampled upon, then this tyranny can happen to anyone. The US government has no qualms in garnishing my overseas wages for tax revenue, but yet I myself, am not welcome back in the country. My tax money is welcomed (demanded) back in America, but I as a US citizen and military veteran am not welcome back to my own country. I have been detained, searched, humiliated, interrogated, surveilled, deceived, and assaulted by the US government. I have been treated as a persona non grata, and therefore I am not interested in returning to or being associated with a country that does not honor and respect its citizens, especially its military veterans.

As the moral fabric of America continues to erode and the tyrannical globalist authority of the US government and US corporations continue to subjugate the citizens into an ever increasingly dysfunctional and dystopian society, a new form of dissident leadership will need to return, one that is based on protecting the individual freedoms of American Citizens, as well as putting the patriotic pride of America and the love of country first. To all American patriots, this is a muster call. We have been betrayed by the enemies within our own country. In these pages I provide details of the betrayal and explain the type of leadership required for success.

Just as the Roman Empire fell, so too America has already been in decline, and this predicament will continue to get even worse. Americans can no longer afford to put their trust in either the US government or US corporations. By understanding the principles of leadership, you will realize that the only places US citizens should put their trust are with faith, family, and freedom. Join me on this journey through leadership and betrayal.

You do not need to be a rebel to be a leader, however, a leader must have the courage to rebel.

1

New York Upbringing

I was born Ryan David Baumblatt in Westchester County, New York. I am the son of a New York Jewish-American father and a German-American Immigrant mother. My father served in the US Navy and is a proud veteran who frequently reminded me and my older brother, Jon, that he and our uncle never got drafted to go to Vietnam. On the contrary, they both volunteered as they believed it was their patriotic duty to serve in the military—just as generations had done before.

My family hails from the warrior class on both my mother's and father's sides. My extended family is full of military veterans, firefighters, and law enforcement officers. During World War II, both my Jewish-American grandfather and my German grandfather were both volunteer soldiers who fought for their own respective sides during the war, giving me a unique perspective on WWII.

My forefathers on my father's side first immigrated to America back in the 1850s; they were Ashkenazi Jews from Bavaria, Germany. My great-great-grandfather Joseph Beckhardt, upon immigrating to New York City, volunteered to fight in the American Civil War and served as a captain in the Union calvary. His officer saber is still an heirloom in our family. Tradition has it that Joseph Beckhardt was proud to be able to serve in the military of his adopted country that was the epitome of freedom and opportunity. My father always viewed America's greatest strength as its freedoms.

Our family was politically independent, although conservative leaning. We did not grow up with any strict religious beliefs, however, God was always a part of our lives. Having attended Shabbats and Chabads randomly throughout the years, I have now formally embraced Judaism. Having previously utilized my middle name of David when communicating only with the Rabbis during Synagogue, I now prefer to use my name David with everyone, as well as to also embrace my family roots by using my original family name of Baumblatt. My father, who can best be described as the Jewish version of Archie Bunker, was an old-school American patriot and entrepreneur. After leaving the military, my father, who is not a fan of liberal colleges, decided to focus on learning a blue-collar trade. He became fond of horticulture and started his own tree business, which involved pruning, spraying, climbing, chopping down trees, and such. He enjoyed the work because it involved natural surroundings, manual labor, and certain danger operating heavy chainsaws and climbing trees. In fact, one time my father severely broke his leg when it got pinned between a tree and a falling log. His long road to recovery put a huge financial stress on the family. My father was tough and handled it like a man. The family recovered fine through his leadership. My mother was a homemaker and often reminded my brother and I that the happiest time of her life was when Jon and I were little children, as she could play, cuddle, and care for us all day long. She idolized motherhood and frequently recalled all the wonderful times she had at being a mother.

When I was ten years old, my father being an avid outdoorsman. He loved hunting and fishing, so much he moved our family from

Westchester to the Catskills in upstate New York. There I grew up on a small farm with horses. My father started his second business: a nursery landscaping business, which was similar to his tree business he had sold in Westchester, New York.

Upstate New York was a different culture and different people than Westchester. Some of the local people targeted my Jewish Father with some colorful language. As a result, my father decided to shorten our last name to Baum in the hopes of fitting in better with the local culture. My father never complained and would never tolerate accepting a victim mentality. Every time my father received some colorful words from the locals, he displayed no fear in replying to the locals with his own choice of colorful words. He would say this many times, "This is what freedom is all about; they can say what they want, and I can say what I want. I'm a veteran. I earned that right."

My father was very proud of his veteran status and always gave preferential treatment to other veterans no matter what type of person they were. "They are veterans, and they deserve respect," he would say. My father would sometimes show my brother and I pictures of his time in the US Navy. It was the best decision in his life to volunteer to serve in the military. He is a proud American; however, he has also lost faith in the liberal globalist direction America is going.

While in the Catskills, I enjoyed participating in Cub Scouts, Webelos, and Boy Scouts; as all these organizations provided young boys with many opportunities to learn about the outdoors, leadership, and patriotism.

It is a shame that the current state of Boy Scouts is like the current state of America; they are both in decline. Boy Scouts is a true leadership gem for young boys; so sad to see it deteriorate. I grew up very patriotic and was enamored with the military stories that I was fortunate to hear in the conversations my father had with his veteran friends. In my bedroom hung an American flag with an eagle and a banner on it. The banner read "America, Love it or Leave it." I remember that flag vividly and have never forgotten what leadership principle that flag was imparting: *Lead, Follow, or Get Out of the Way.*

Since elementary school, I always knew I wanted to serve in the military. The calling ran deep in me. When I entered junior high, my plan was to enlist in the US Marine Corps. I had always wanted to become a Marine. During my high school days, however, I had many questions about the process and what life was like in the military. I would ask friends and acquaintances who had recently joined or were in the military about their experiences. I occasionally had the opportunity to speak with military recruiters, but they didn't visit the small, country towns very often.

On one occasion I met a high school student who was enlisting in the Marine Corps. He told me that since I had leadership credentials, such as Eagle Scout, Boy's State, captain of varsity sports, vice president of student council, and president of Students Against Drunk Driving, I should consider going into the Marine Corps as an officer, as opposed to an enlisted Marine. At first, I did not understand what the difference between an officer and an enlisted member was. I had to go to college and enroll in Reserve Officer Training Corps (ROTC) for the Marines to be an officer. The whole process of ROTC sounded confusing to me, as I didn't understand why I needed to go to college when I just wanted to go into the Marine Corps. He told me to talk to my guidance counselor. My guidance counselor told me if I was interested in becoming a Marine Corps officer, I should apply to the US Naval Academy.

"What is the Naval Academy?" I asked.

He smirked. "It is where the best Naval and Marine Corps officers graduate. It's very prestigious," he said. It sounded very prestigious, and I intently listened to him as he proceeded to walk me through a US Naval Academy catalog. I was fascinated with the idea of attending the Naval Academy and becoming a Marine Corps officer. He then asked, "Have you also thought about West Point?"

"What is West Point?" I asked.

"West Point is where the best Army officers graduate." He then handed me an official West Point catalog.

I took the catalogs home and read and reread the West Point catalogue at least ten times, after which I felt certain my life's calling was to graduate from West Point and become an Army officer. I wanted to follow in the footsteps of the Long Gray Line (the West Point Alumni) who have shaped the history of America and also the world. I was now on a mission; I would become a West Pointer.

During my senior year in high school, I applied to West Point. Several months later, I received a letter from the academy informing me that my application was rejected. The letter contained standard wording of how competitive it is and that the academy receives thousands of applications every year. They regretfully informed me that I would not be granted admission, but they did provide instructions on how I could reapply the next year and also provided a list of various military preparatory schools to which I should apply in order to increase my chances of acceptance into West Point the following year. I immediately decided that I was not going to give up on my dream to attend West Point; I planned to reapply the following year, and in the meantime I decided to apply to Marion Military Institute (MMI), a two-year junior military college located in Marion, Alabama.

MMI is America's oldest military junior college and was named after the Revolutionary War Hero Brigadier General Francis Marion, who was infamously known by the British as the Swamp Fox, a true American patriot portrayed in the Mel Gibson movie *The Patriot*. Francis Marion's use of irregular guerrilla warfare against the British has led him to be considered the father of American Military Special Operations. I was thrilled to be accepted by MMI and was lucky enough to receive an Army ROTC scholarship. After my high school graduation, I shipped off to begin my training. First I went to Fort Knox, Kentucky, to complete the Army ROTC Basic Camp and then I reported to MMI to begin my cadet training. While at MMI, I was enrolled in both the West Point preparatory program as well as Army ROTC.

My cadet experience at MMI was memorable to say the least. Unlike West Point, which is under the strict spotlight of political oversight and media attention, MMI is a much smaller, less regulated, and lesser-known military school. Some of the entering new cadets at MMI, did not enter because they wanted to become top-notch Army officers. Some of them were troubled young men, and their parents thought that sending their young sons to a military school to learn discipline would not only improve their lives but also decrease the chances of them becoming full-fledged delinquents and thus having a future involving drugs, prison, unemployment, or some other unfortunate outcome. The physical hazing at MMI would sometimes lead to all-out beat downs, blanket parties, fights, and brawls; the upper-class cadets at MMI could get away with much more than those at West Point.

At West Point the hazing focused on tremendous amount of pressure poured on cadets on a daily basis. The cadet's mission was to either meet the standards or else be dismissed from West Point. At MMI, however, the hazing involved racial slurs, profanity, and old-fashion fisticuffs. Looking back, I actually smile and laugh at my time at MMI. Sometimes that old-school leadership training will never go out of style—maybe something today's West Point could use more of to break it free from the progressive politics and path of liberal wokeness, which is resulting in weak and clueless West Point graduates.

When I moved to Alabama from New York, it almost felt like I was in a different country. Unlike West Point where the Corps of Cadets is made up of young Americans evenly representing the entire USA, the majority of cadets at MMI came from Alabama and the nearby southern states. The MMI cadets called me Yankee, a term that I thought had died out; apparently it was still alive in Alabama. In fact, Rocco, the Italian Stallion from Philadelphia, also got called a Yankee.

Rocco was one of those troubled kids I described earlier. His mother sent him to MMI in the hopes that he would stay out of trouble. The very first time I met Rocco was in the MMI barracks during the first week of our arrival. His shirt was all bloody as he just got done putting a beat down on another cadet. Rocco's father was an Italian mafia hitman and was actually on the FBI's most wanted list for all his murders. I had the opportunity to meet his father once; he seemed like a nice gentleman. He is currently in prison, serving a life's sentence for murder.

There was also another cadet classmate named Vincent; we all called him Psycho Vincent because he constantly told us how he couldn't wait to go to war and finally be able to kill people. We all assumed he was referring to kill enemy soldiers as opposed to people in general, but we were never quite sure. Along with his extensive collection of combat knives, Psycho Vincent was also a gun nut who would make the National Rifle Association very proud. He always took great pleasure in showing off his private arsenal of assault rifles, which he stored right in his cadet room.

Finally, there was Cadet Trask. Due to his unhygienic grooming standards and messy room conditions, we all referred to him as Trash Can Man or just Trash for short. Trash certainly had his difficulties in keeping proper uniform, room, and even his own bodily hygiene up to MMI Standards. One time when his facial acne flared up something bad. Being in a military school probably served him well as us fellow cadets were forced to hang around him. If Trash had gone to a civilian college, many of us probably would have avoided him out of concern for our own personal health and welfare. Despite the no smoking policy at MMI, Trash Can Man perfected the stealthy method of being able to smoke in the barracks and not get caught. When cadets needed contraband cigarettes, Trash Can Man always had a supply.

What I liked most about MMI was that it was more raw than West Point. For example, West Point Sunday services were optional; however, at MMI it was mandatory. And there was definitely not a Jewish Synagogue in Marion, Alabama, so it was Christian Church for me. I was fine with it. Sometimes I miss that old, conservative, traditional way of America. MMI leadership had no problem with mixing God and leadership. That would be politically unacceptable at today's West Point.

MMI cadets could do things that would never be tolerated at the more politically correct West Point. For example, most of the MMI cadets hailed from southern states and would proudly hang the Confederate flag in their rooms or on their cars and would yell out loud "the South will rise again!" when they saw Yankees like me and

Rocco passing by. We would reply, "We Beat you Rednecks!" We took it all in good fun. They meant no hate; they were just proud of their Southern heritage, and good for them. The conservative traditions of the American South have a lot to teach the rest of liberal America.

My English Professor at MMI was Colonel (retired) Young. We all referred to him as Ranger Young as he was a former US Army Ranger, and also a West Point graduate. Ranger Young was absolutely hardcore and old-school. Ranger Young spoke his mind and was completely shameless. During his English classes, he would purposely and frequently steer the class discussion toward his political and leadership views. He would say that women do not belong in the military or talk about how weak and undisciplined today's American young men are. He was also a great admirer of Germany and anything German. His behavior never would have been tolerated at West Point, but that is why we liked him. Many cadets thought that Ranger Young was a Nazi. I thought that Ranger Young was not only a great English professor. More important, he truly cared about the physical, academic, and moral development of the MMI Cadets. He was an American patriot and a great role model for young American men.

At MMI, if you had a problem with someone, you said it directly to their face. If neither of you backed down, then the rumble would begin. We are missing this leadership trait in America—that sense of rawness. As the political animosities continue to boil up in America, the citizens are becoming ever more angry at not being allowed to openly express our true feelings. That's not how it was at MMI. Cadets like Rocco the Italian Stallion, Psycho Vincent, and Trash Can Man, as well as professors like Ranger Young, taught us that much needed raw character development which is so lacking in today's American men. Military schools sometimes have an eerie similarity to the prison system with their survival of the fittest and a dominance hierarchy culture. Military schools are not fun places, and every cadet yearns for the time when they graduate. Despite the harshness, the lasting memories, leadership lessons, and lifelong friendships make the experience one of the most amazing on a young man's life. I did have some hard times at MMI, and I want to thank two mentors: Brigadier General Walter Kastenmayer and Lieutenant Colonel David Bauer. Both of these gentlemen were my professors and mentors at MMI, and they both helped me get into West Point. As was the case with my scout master; the selfless service that General Kastenmayer showed me was truly heartwarming. He took the time to tutor me before classes so that I could raise my grades in order to increase my chances for acceptance into West Point. I remember thinking, "Why is this guy getting up so early in the morning to tutor me; isn't he tired, why is he helping me?" I was truly blown away with his concern and care for me.

Midway through my first year at MMI I submitted my application to West Point for a second time. Unlike my first application, this one was much stronger; not only did I have an additional year of experience at the junior military college and Army ROTC on my application, this time I also was also able to successfully gain a congressional nomination to West Point from my US Congressman from New York State. My hopes were high, but yet again, West Point informed me that my second application was also rejected. Depression ensued; my dream was crushed.

The summer after my first year at MMI, I completed the Army ROTC Advanced Camp in Fort Lewis, Washington. I then entered my second and final year at MMI as an upper-class cadet with plans to graduate MMI and complete my Army ROTC training. During my second year at MMI, I decided to reapply to West Point for a third and final time; just one more chance to achieve my dream.

At the end of the spring semester of my second year at MMI, as graduation approached and I facing a second lieutenant (2LT) commission via Army ROTC, word finally came back from West Point regarding my application. To my sheer amazement, I was accepted. The cadet education system at MMI proved to be a success. Not only did MMI teach me how to become a leader and a US Army Officer, it also was instrumental in me getting accepted into the US Military Academy and thus attaining my dream of becoming a West Pointer. Thank you, MMI, "Bold Tigers!"

Upon receipt of my acceptance letter to West Point, I informed Army ROTC Cadet Command of my situation. A few weeks after my MMI graduation, I received another letter from West Point addressed to 2LT David Baumblatt. They informed me that when I report to West Point, I would first need to report to the military personal records office where I would be decommissioned from a second lieutenant back down to a cadet. During my decommissioning ceremony at West Point, the officer in charge told me that according to their records, I was the twelfth person in the history of America to ever begin admissions into West Point after having already been commissioned as an officer in the US Military. My four years at West Point could easily fill a book by itself. I will focus, however, on one aspect of West Point Leadership that all cadets experience at the academy: hand-to-hand combat.

To Become a Leader;
You Must Learn How to Fight

A leader does not necessarily need to be a fighter, but a leader must be able to fight. Sooner or later you will be confronted with adversity and adversaries. Sometimes these hardships and battles will be relatively easy to overcome. Other times they may pit you up against your very own survival. A leader must be able to summon the courage and strength to fight for his beliefs and defend himself and his people. By learning how to physically fight in hand-to-hand combat the leader develops the mental and physical fortitude required to increase his chances of survival and victory on the battlefield and in the boardroom. Before entering West Point, I had already attained proficiency level at Chinese boxing. This is a form of Wing Chun (咏春)[1] and therefore I was eager at stepping into the Boxing Ring; and learning the "sweet science". West Point has three levels of boxing: plebe boxing, voluntary intramural boxing, and competitive collegiate boxing. Plebe boxing is a semester-long class taken during your first year. It teaches cadets the fundamentals of boxing and culminates into four graded boxing bouts. In order to receive the minimum passing score, the plebes must exhibit the following two basic actions during their graded boxing bouts:

1. The Plebe must not run from his opponent. He must stand his ground and fight. Yes, he may bob and weave, circle back and forth, and duck and cover, but he must not retreat. He is required to engage the enemy. He must overcome whatever fear he has, and he must not retreat from combat.

2. The plebe must deliver his maximum amount of capable force to destroy his enemy. This force will be channeled through the plebes fists, thereby punching his opponent with the full intent and action to knock him out. The plebe must learn to accept and embrace violence of action as a means to win combat.

All West Point graduates fondly remember their plebe boxing experience, and it was at West Point that I personally fell in love with boxing. Upon the successful completion of plebe boxing, I went on to represent my cadet company D1—Go Ducks!—in the intramural boxing competitions. Together the D1 boxing team won the West Point Brigade Boxing Intramural Championships. After Intramural Boxing, I then went on to become the heavyweight boxer of the West Point Collegiate Boxing Team and eventually become the co-captain of the boxing team.

Later in my military career, when I was stationed in Baumholder, Germany, I would go on to become the two-time US All-Armed Forces European Heavyweight Boxing Champion. The professional boxer, Ray Mercer, was also a former soldier who was stationed in Baumholder as well. He had won the US All Armed Forces European heavyweight title too. I was the number-two ranked heavyweight boxer in the US Army, with a slot to fight for number one. My desire was to fight for the chance to make the Olympic team; however, an intimate leadership evolution had other plans for me. This evolution allowed me to learn some deep lessons in human nature, which included betrayal and deceit, promulgated yet again by the corrupt FBI. That is a story for another time.

All that time I had spent in the Boxing Ring provided me with many leadership lessons. I never forgot about mentorship and selfless service; therefore, later in my life, I transitioned into volunteering as a boxing coach for young men. I was the Assistant Boxing Coach for both the University of San Francisco's and Harvard University's Boxing Teams. While in China, I opened up my own boxing club after I received notoriety for being the assistant boxing coach to the first ever Chinese World Boxing Champion. On 24 November 2012, Xiong

Zhao Zhong (熊朝忠)[2] became the first boxer from China to win a major professional world boxing title, the WBC Mini-Flyweight Title.

Boxing also followed me into the FBI, where FBI new agent trainees (NATs) are required to undergo a mandatory boxing program, which culminates into fight day called the Bull in the Ring. The new agent is required to stand in the middle of a circle, while he is surrounded by his fellow NATs. One by one, each NAT enters the circle and engages with the defending NAT by unleashing around fifteen seconds of uninterrupted violent punches. By the time the last NAT enters the circle, the original defending NAT is barely able to hold his gloves up to properly defend and protect himself.

Boxing pushes the leader to his physical limits; and teaches him to take a punch and to give a punch, to survive the attack, and take the pain. When I was the co-captain of the West Point Boxing Team, my coach would sometimes ask me if I would volunteer my time to help give a struggling plebe cadet additional boxing instruction. One particular plebe was in danger of failing his mandatory plebe boxing course, which would have resulted in his dismissal from West Point. What one learns in the evolution of leadership is that fear is probably the biggest limiting factor in one's development, and in boxing, fear can catapult to the front of a young man's psyche. That was exactly the case with this plebe. He had been knocked out in his previous plebe boxing match and following the usual doctor and medical checks, he was on his way back to recovery. Thus he was now required to repeat the plebe boxing class. However, he dreaded stepping back in the ring. I told him he had no choice—other than quitting the academy. He needed to complete and pass his boxing course—no excuse and no fear.

He was faced with only two choices: successfully complete the course or leave West Point. When someone is gripped with fear, there are many ways he or she may overcome it, but only he or she can overcome their fear; no one else can. He or She must become their own gallant knight and slay their own dragon or beast. Their sword. Their dragon. Their fear. Their courage.

This evolution of fear and courage is how leaders are made, and Boxing is an essential tool in the path toward achieving knighthood. The plebe in question, by the way, overcame his fear and eventually passed plebe boxing. Although not exactly with flying colors, he ultimately survived that leadership evolution and slayed his dragon. Upon his successful completion of plebe boxing, the smile and happiness he displayed could have brightened a dark dungeon.

This plebe's boxing experience is about human life and leadership. Many times we will not be the best and brightest in the evolutionary battle that we are facing. However, we must at the very minimum survive and pass the test; thus, passing through the gauntlet of fear. Hand-to-hand combat training prepares you for life's challenges and significantly increases your chances of survival by teaching you to have the skills and courage required to first and foremost defeat the most fearsome demon of your entire life: yourself.

What is it that you Wish for;
asked the Son.
To Die an Honorable Man;
replied the Father.

My message to young American men is to go out into the wild and forge your own trail with courage and sweat and earn your own respect with self-reliance and character and become your own warrior leader by slaying your own dragons. Have confidence in yourself. God is with you, and may you always be faithful to him. Focus more on doing the morally right thing and do not be afraid to break the rules. Embrace danger and risk your life and do not be afraid of loneliness. Always remember, sooner or later your life will come to an end. Therefore, learn to live with death by your side and God in your heart. What is mortal rests in the blood of man. Find the immortality of life, which lies in the parallel emptiness of light and darkness. The hand of God is upon you.

Be Open to Learn and You will Be Open to Change. Transform Yourself into the Warrior Who Seeks Wisdom

2

Real World Leadership

Leadership is like nature. There will always be a price that needs to be paid and not everyone will be the winner. Leadership is found in a dangerous world, which is inhabited by brave men of character. Just as a harsh winter gives one thanks for warmth and shelter; so too will chaos and violence give one thanks for strong men of leadership. Hard times are coming, and a great leadership evolution is coming with it. In the conventional sense of statehood, leadership is formed in a pyramidal structure with the heads of economics (leaders of business) and the heads of security (leaders of military) forming the base of the pyramid called the state with the top of the pyramid being the head of state (president).

COUNTRY LEADER (President)

**BUSINESS
LEADERS (CEOs)**

**MILITARY
LEADERS (Generals)**

The head of state is normally the tribe's supreme leader and is one who is the epitome of leadership. The President of the United States, for example, should be the greatest leader in the country. We look to our military generals and corporate CEOs as the base of American leadership and then to the President of the United States as the primary leader, presiding over the base.

The opposite is true today. America's leadership is in decline. America's generals, CEOs, and Presidents have all lost the trust and faith of the American people. Through their weakness, immorality has flourished. Through their selfishness, disloyalty has flourished. Expanding beyond the conventional concept of leadership; the greatest of all leaders in fact, transcend time and space. This is the universal leadership of religion, philosophy, and spirituality. Universal leaders such as Abraham, Moses, Jesus Christ, Lao Tzu, the Buddha, Confucius, and the Prophet Mohammad went above and beyond what the normal definitions of leadership prescribe; however, these heavenly leaders led their followers to salvation beyond the earthly realm. Therefore, the concepts of morality and faith in God and nature go past what any head of state can ever attest to. To truly understand leadership, one must study, embrace, and believe in a higher moral faith. Although I have personally embraced the religious faith of Judaism, even as a Jew, I still include (in my spiritual journey) the philosophical teachings of Chinese Daoism（道教）, which I have been studying since childhood. Although I do not push or advocate for any certain type of religion, spirituality, or philosophy, I do believe every leader must make amends with God and embrace God because without God the leader will never be ethically strong and morally guided.

Regarding America, it was founded on Judeo-Christian beliefs. Therefore, America, like Europe, should be tolerant of all religions, philosophies, and spiritual teaching, but the primary or official religion, philosophy, or spirituality should always remain Judeo-Christianity. The fall of Judeo-Christianity will also be the fall of Western society.

Most of the leadership experts over the past decades have failed to guide America as a nation and people. Whatever advice these so-called experts have pushed, in the end, it has been wrong or seriously lacking. Americans would be better off not following most of this modern leadership advice because the state of America continues to get worse and worse—to the point of collapse. So the question is; what is going wrong?

The first point that the reader must understand is that leadership in general is a dangerous profession, and most of these so-called leaders do not even emulate the type of person who is courageous enough to take on evil. What Americans are told is leadership, in many cases, is not leadership at all. Today's modern leadership courses are more like management courses, teaching students how to become more effective and efficient in their life or job. While management courses are really great and helpful in their own right, they are not to be confused with leadership courses. Allow me to present you with some adjectives that describe the difference between leaders and leadership compared with managers and management:

Leadership Qualities	Management Qualities
Chaos	Control
Ambiguity	Clarity
People	Things
Danger	Safety
Change	Constant
Unconventional	Conventional

Morality	Legality
Principles	Rules
War	Peace
Instability	Stability
Oath	Contract
Trust	Supervision
Brothers	Colleagues
People	Human Capital
Risk Taking	Risk Adverse
God	Government
Weird	Normal
Freedom	Restraint
Playful	Serious
Rule Breaker	Rule Follower
Insubordinate	Subordinate
Influence	Authority
Flexible	Regimented
Wacky	Mundane
Misunderstood	Understood
Creative	Uncreative
Rebel	Conformist
Sensitive	Insensitive
Heart	Head
Relationships	Networking
Intuition	Reasoning

In society, both leaders and managers are needed and are both important. The point is not to paint a picture of either leaders or managers being better or more important than the other. Like yin and yang (阴阳) [1] both qualities are part of nature. While many managers and leaders may have a mix of both sets of the above qualities, what is important to know is that the qualities of management and leadership are not the same. Some people will be more aligned to leadership and others more aligned to management. To better understand the comparison between the two I will use both military and business analogies in the following examples:

- **Military Management**: Training bootcamp is a system where new recruits report to military basic training and within a matter of months they become fully indoctrinated into military life; the scope and process of their military transformation is clear and ordered. Success is defined by the new recruits meeting all the defined standards by graduation in order for them to become fully qualified and credentialed as soldiers. Think of the drill sergeants as the highly adept military managers.

- **Military Leadership**: Battlefield combat is a violent and chaotic clash between two opposing forces which usually results in deadly consequences; the scope and process is ambiguous and unstable. Success is defined by the enemy being killed, captured, or forced into retreat. Key terrain is seized and enemy assets are destroyed or confiscated. There is generally no top management supervision present during combat. Battlefield decisions are made in real time by the commanders on the ground, and the pace is so fast that the reptilian limbic brain overtakes intellectual rationale judgement with respect to decision making. Battlefield commanders are highly adept military leaders.

- **Business Management**: Production factories are systems where raw materials and/or parts are assembled within a set timeframe and set standard. The inspected finished products are ready for market; the scope and process are clear and ordered. Success is defined by the finished products meeting the defined output target standards relative to time, quality, quantity, costs, safety, environment, and personnel. Factory supervisors are highly adept business managers.

- **Business Leadership**: Marketing brings new products or services to an unknown foreign target sector where already established competitors exist; the scope and process is ambiguous, unstable, and risky. Success is defined by the competitors being destroyed or marginalized—pushed out of the market. When this happens, the new market is seized, and the new customer segment is captured—and increased profits are realized. Think of the regional sales managers as the highly adept business leaders.

As you may have already guessed; being a competent leader versus a competent manager takes a different set of skills. Few people are naturally adapted to do both—and, of course, many people cannot do either. There is a saying in the military:

Peace time generals make good managers.
War time generals make good leaders.

The environment is a big factor in developing leaders versus managers. Hence, naturally gravitating toward one's suitable industry, department, team, culture, market, or country is important to make a good fit for aspiring leaders or managers.

- Using Physics, leadership would be defined as a vector (force and direction). The leader dictates the direction, and the driving force are the people. A leader knows that people are his most essential element. Without people, the leader is nothing. The leader utilizes the energy of his people to create a driving force, thus propelling the group into new horizons. The key is to take the group toward new territory or higher levels, and to accomplish this mission, the leader ultimately relies on his people to give him the energy needed.

- Using Geometry, management would be defined as a circle (enclosed and repetitive). The manager is responsible for controlling a system. Although he/she strives to make the system more effective and efficient, he/she is still confined to this circular contained system. The system has various inputs such as time, money, equipment, people, or information. A manager regards people as just one of many business inputs as opposed to a leader who regards people as the most essential element.

So why are today's leadership experts *not* delivering leadership advisory to their customers? Today's leadership advice is not helping America and Americans as a whole get better. On the contrary, America is getting worse and worse. Even most of today's political leaders, military generals, business leaders, and even religious leaders are utterly failing in steering the American ship to safe harbor. The situation in America is getting more dire. So the question again is: Where are the leadership experts? Why aren't the leaders delivering results? The answer is a combination of competence, fear, and greed:

1. Most so-called leaders have no "real-world" experience in leadership. Their understanding of leadership is based on second-hand knowledge and/or academic thesis.

2. Most so-called leaders are afraid to speak the truth and purposely avoid taking a stand for faith, family, and freedom. These experts are afraid to offend their audience and risk hindering their career.

3. Most so-called leaders do not want to jeopardize their revenues and businesses by standing for the truth. Therefore, they present whatever idea their constituents are willing to buy.

The result at the end of these leadership instructions is that the audience gets politically correct, atheistic neutral, non-practical, "warm and fuzzy" theories or pep talks on how to become a better person or team—or how to become a better worker bee for the corporation. This type of theoretical training does not prepare them for the real world. In the end the person, the team, or the country as a whole, is lulled into a false sense of leadership until sooner or later everyone is faced with reality and survival mode when they face real stress. This is what is happening in America. More and more Americans are realizing the lukewarm "Chicken Soup for the Soul" leadership lectures they have been receiving for decades are not helping them, their families, their organizations, or even the country. It is just not working.

Sooner or later, all Americans will wake up to their harsh new reality. Even though I left America in 2010, I already saw America's bleak future; I do not advocate leaving one's country as the best solution. I do, however, urge Americans to dispense from accepting the politically correct and atheistic neutral language of leadership and embrace the hard uncensored reality:

Hard Times are Coming for America, but the Good News is Strong Men will be Coming as Well.

Let us now look more into the relationship between fear and leadership. Most godless people live their lives based on choosing the life path, which will offer them the greatest amount of safety and security; most people are naturally risk adverse. People who have embraced god in their lives will choose a principled path that leads them to salvation, and they will welcome the unavoidable risks associated with it. As a former FBI agent, my choice to leave the Bureau meant I was leaving a very prestigious and financially rewarding government career. However, I put my faith in God and chose ethics above job security. My morals and passions were not in line with that agency.

I challenge law enforcement officers and FBI agents who continue to enforce immoral laws and regulations, the same old excuse of "I am just following orders," is not valid. As a former FBI agent, I put my morals and values above my career aspirations and job security. I had the courage to quit the FBI and leave an immoral law enforcement agency. So should you. You have the freedom to decide whether or not you will to put God's law above that of your job security. The highest oath a man can take is with God, and in the end, there will be no excuse as to why he did something or failed to do something. God has granted man with free will, and with it comes the ultimate power of self-determination. In the end, ultimately we will all be judged by God and God alone.

To all American leaders, whether in the public or private sectors, no one has forced you to become a leader; the choice was yours and yours alone. And with it comes responsibility. At any time, you have the free will to stand down, to quit your job, to leave your organization, or even to leave your own country as I did. If your morality doesn't align with your organization's culture and actions, then I urge you to remember that no one is forcing you to carry out any order or forcing you to stay in your organization or company.

The level of fear in America has gotten so high that people are so afraid to speak what is on their minds. The notion of freedom of speech is becoming obsolete as saying what is truly on your mind can have grave consequences for your career or even your personal safety. Leaders, therefore, choose not to give the full truth and continue down the path of politically correct speech. This is where former President Donald Trump deserves much credit. His courage to speak with more open frankness to the realities facing America is commendable, whereas most other politicians were too afraid to talk about it. He singlehandedly changed the political discourse in America regarding sensitive topics like the border (build the wall) to mainstream conversation points.

The main reason why leadership is failing in America is that we are afraid to talk about important topics like race, gender, sexuality, religion, and immigration. Telling the truth about these subjects is just too dangerous. Leadership advice today is lacking in raw candor. The real truth is concealed, and glossed over with niceties, so in the end, everyone feels good and no one is offended. Freedom of speech is the most important freedom we have; never take it for granted. Always be ready to defend this right should others threaten to take it away. Without free speech, there is no free thought and then even your own mind will be governed and controlled by those in power.

Without Freedom of Speech There Is No Democracy

As a young man, I volunteered to serve my country so that its citizens could continue to enjoy their constitutional freedoms and ultimately be able to speak their minds regardless if those listening agree or disagree with their viewpoints. Without free speech, there is no freedom. The American people are desperate for leaders who have the courage to speak up against the growing oppression of their individual freedoms and patriotic culture, an oppression coming from their very own government that instead of serving and protecting its citizens prefers to serve the godless globalist corporations instead. As more and more Americans experience government oppression, a strategic change is needed for American leadership. Otherwise, the American system will violently collapse. It is time for Americans to openly question and challenge their government in the way they are currently being governed, otherwise what is most cherished in the American way of life may be permanently jeopardized and lost forever.

Faith, Family, Freedom

Looking back on my life, some of the greatest leadership experiences that had the biggest impact on me were those that taught me self-reliance. We live mortal lives and our time on this earth is short. We will ultimately be judged for our actions and inactions while on this earth. Seeking knowledge is our best asset in the negotiation and understanding of the world around us. Our minds are our greatest weapon. Below are three facets of life that changed me the most as a person and increased my leadership capabilities. These three facets sadly may not be viable for most young American men today, as the family unit has already been destroyed and the US Military has become incompetent and immoral. Perhaps then only the third facet may be useful as the percentage of American citizens leaving the United States continues to increase year by year:

Childhood mentors. The first biggest factor in my leadership evolution were my childhood mentors. This is probably common with almost all people. Whether it was your parents, close friends, teachers, or some other mentor. The leadership lessons imparted on young adults are so significance in the later years. I was fortunate to have a great father and other male role models like my scout master, Denny, as well as my older brother, Jon. What is lacking in today's society are positive male role models and mentors for young boys. As mentioned above, with the destruction of the American family and community, the whole concept of a "childhood home" is turning into a fleeting memory for modern-day Americans. Destroy the family, destroy the community, destroy the home, and the result will be the destruction of America.

Military service. The second biggest factor in my leadership evolution was joining the military. In many ways it is like entering another world, one that is so far apart from the civilian world. It is a world where individual rights and freedoms are taken away, and this new soldier must always put the team before himself. It is a life of discipline and hardship, but it also a rewarding life. You are part of something bigger than yourself and also being part of a team that is like family. You learn brotherhood and loyalty. You hone your warrior spirit and overcome fear in the face of danger. You learn the tenets of mission and what it takes to achieve victory. The environment is very homogenous, however, operating on a global and international level. It is an experience that only military veterans can understand and appreciate; it will change your life. It changed mine. Although, with today's unethical and weak military officer corps already having become a tool for American globalist corporations and elites, I do not recommend young Americans join the military. My advice to active-duty military is to focus on defending the Constitution and the right to freedom of speech.

Overseas travel. The third biggest factor in my leadership evolution was my overseas travel experiences, especially living overseas. Before one is confident to declare what is good or bad about their country, one needs to have real-world experience, so they have the relevant knowledge in which to compare their country with others. Traveling and living in foreign countries will give you direct experience that will challenge many of your own cultural biases. The more foreign of a country, the greater the leadership evolution will be. For example, an American living in the UK won't have as much of a cultural education as an American living in India where their customs and beliefs are radically different. This was of course my experience when I lived in Europe as compared to when I lived in Asia. Asia was much more foreign to me, and thus the learning curve being much steeper.

In order to really understand what you are and what you believe, you must put yourself in environments that challenge your identity, outlook, and morals. Leadership is in many ways the study of physics, the yin and the yang; these opposing forces are needed, and sometimes in the great Dao, or great order of the universe or god. Sometimes neither force is right or wrong in the grand universe as they are both needed to collide and battle with each other to create something even greater and more profound than themselves. The product of this cosmic collision is the new birth of the duality of nature, a new leadership evolution that guides people yet again to the next stage of human evolution until the next human conflict occurs.

As a leader, you must be a fighter and you must enjoy the fight, but always remember, we are god's children. We may never know the mysterious bigger picture of the world or the true wisdom of the universe. Many times we are stuck in short-range occupied combat while forgetting the long-range evolutionary strategy; only God knows, and we can only attempt to understand his message.

As God will forgive; so too should man learn to forgive others; as we are all sometimes ignorant of the grand scheme of the universe; we are still in many ways children, trying to understand God's greater plan. As mortal men we should act in accordance to forgiveness, but when the bell rings, we must be ready to fight. Combat is part of man's calling, and through combat the evolution of leadership is allowed to grow and foster to new insights into man's place on this earth and in heaven.

Crisis and Opportunity （危机）[2]

Agonizing disaster will lead to defeat.

Embracing disaster will lead to victory.

3

FBI's Treason

The FBI's unconstitutional spying on me—specifically their targeting me because of my conservative political views—is the primary motivation for me to write this book. Before I begin, however, I would first like to address current and former FBI agents, as well as FBI support employees. To my former colleagues, I am proud to state that the FBI hails in American history as an awe-inspiring organization shrouded in power and secrecy whose primary purpose is to protect and defend America, American citizens, and the American way of life. I was truly humbled to have been accepted into the FBI and join the ranks of one of America's most hollowed government agencies. I know many honorable FBI agents who wear their badge on their hearts—and for which the FBI is even a family legacy. The pride that you have for the FBI is commendable. I also have had many personal interactions with FBI agents who are truly the salt of the earth, who have helped and mentored me. I am grateful for your kindness and friendship. Therefore, it brings me no joy in publicly criticizing your admired FBI. My plan was always to keep my silence about the corruption within FBI management.

After my departure from the bureau in 2007, except for a personal letter I wrote to then Senator Grassley detailing the immoral conduct that I witnessed on the part of FBI management, I have never talked about my FBI experiences to the public—nor do I even talk about it with family, friends, or colleagues. Almost all of my colleagues, acquaintances, contacts, and friends don't even know that I have ever served in the FBI. I made the decision when I left the FBI to specifically end that chapter of my life right then and there and to just move on and make a new life for myself. Despite my desire to move on from the FBI, the FBI management has had other plans in store for me. They have continued to spy on me, put my life in danger, and have sabotaged my career on multiple occasions. It is the FBI management who is unwilling to move on and therefore I must now defend myself as a West Point graduate to protect the reputation and legacy of the US Military Academy, as well as that of my family name.

When I was a cadet at West Point, I remember taking a field trip to the New York City FBI field office and was very impressed with what I saw. In the field office I got to meet FBI agents who were also West Point graduates; the experience was awesome. During my time in the Army I was able to meet other FBI agents who were also West Pointers. One in particular was Dan, who served as a great role model for me; however, after ten years as a field agent in the bureau, he too left due to his misgivings with FBI management. Also, I want to thank Brian, who as part of senior management hopefully is an exception to my negative view on bureau management. I remember the time when I was interviewing with the bureau in Philadelphia, and you came to see me and offered me advice. You took me out shooting, and we talked about leadership and the bureau. You were nothing less than absolutely professional. I am very happy to hear about your successful career in the FBI. You bring great credit and honor to both the FBI and West Point. Finally, I want to thank another Brian who is also part of the FBI senior management. As agents, Brian and I had some earlier morning boxing sessions together and he personally invited me into his home and family. Brian—once a Marine always a Marine—never forget your oath to the brotherhood, the corps, and your country. I am glad to see that you are part of FBI management, congratulations, and Semper Fi.

When I entered the FBI Academy at Quantico as a New Agent Trainee (NAT), I was extremely motivated at the opportunity to join such a prestigious agency and also to be able to continue to serve my country. However, my feelings immediately started changing with some of the things I witnessed at the academy. My first impression at Quantico was the clear lack of strong leadership compared to the military. During my training I had an encounter with one of my instructors that left me speechless.

Hogan's Alley is a mock town located on the FBI Academy grounds. It is where role playing exercises occur between the FBI NATs and the FBI civilian support actors, employees who play-act various roles like criminals, terrorists, suspects, bystanders, witnesses, and victims. These exercises are to give the NATs practical simulations to test their ability in employing FBI tradecraft. These practical exercises also allow FBI instructors the chance to evaluate the NATs' performance in simulated exercise environments. Overall, the training in Hogan's Alley is very impressive and essential for the NATs development. However, during one encounter what the training did not include was moral leadership.

For this exercise in particular, my instructor had briefed me about a crime that had recently occurred, and my job was to go investigate the matter. After the briefing I received from the instructor, I chose to go on foot, walking the streets of Hogan's Alley in search of the suspect involved in the criminal matter. While walking on the sidewalk

I encountered a civilian (FBI civilian actor); I knew this person was not the suspect I was searching for; however, I hoped he could provide me with some information to help me with my investigation. Therefore, I approached the civilian and identified myself as a special agent with the FBI (showing him my badge). I then informed him that I was conducting an investigation and was searching for a suspect who was last seen in the vicinity. I asked this person if he was willing to answer my questions and then I specifically and directly informed him that he was under no obligation to answer any of my questions. I told him he was free to refuse to speak with me and was free to go at any time he wished. During this entire encounter, my FBI instructor was right behind me evaluating my performance. After I received the pedestrian's oral consent, I began to conduct my interview. After about five minutes of questions and answers, I wrote down the information he provided me. After that, I thanked him for his time, and we both parted ways. As I was about to walk away, I heard the FBI instructor behind me say, "Hold up Baumblatt!" I turned around to face him. The instructor was both annoyed and perplexed by my actions. "Why did you tell the pedestrian he was not obligated to answer any of your questions?" he asked.

Because he was not obligated to, I thought. "I just wanted him to know that it was voluntary," I told the instructor.

The FBI instructor shook his head at me in disgust. He said, "you never tell them their rights unless you have to; never give away our power, do you understand."

"Yes," I replied.

"That was just stupid," he said. He then shook his head in dismay and disbelief and walked away. I was left stunned. What that FBI instructor just told me was so far removed from my prior military training. I just could not process it morally. In real life, if the pedestrian were a foreign national, then I would happen to agree with this FBI instructor. However, with the case of US citizens, what this instructor told me was just shocking. In the military, we are reminded repeatedly that we are in service to our country, that we are expected to fight and die so that American citizens can live free. American citizens are the taxpayers who fund and support our government agencies; we ultimately work for them. American citizens are the "owners" and "supervisors" of the US government. The government works at the behest of the American people. As an FBI agent I would frequently remind myself that when dealing with US citizens I was to conduct myself as if I were speaking to my supervisor. Many times, US citizens are ignorant of their legal and constitutional rights when dealing with US law enforcement; and US law enforcement will intentionally take advantage of this ignorance to the detriment of the US citizen. This is just absolute treason and immoral leadership on the part of US law enforcement.

Policemen used to be the heroes of the community. Now they are the bullies of the government.

In the military, we define the primary enemy as foreign countries, foreign militaries, and foreign actors. During my time in the FBI, I was lucky that my investigations focused on foreign nationals; however, most FBI and law enforcement agencies investigate US citizens as opposed to foreign nationals. I witnessed an FBI culture that looks upon US citizens as the enemy, the bad guys, the corrupt, the criminals, the gangs, the mafia, the fraudsters, the perpetrators, the cheaters, the crooks. After years and years of being a police officer and having to deal with the "bad elements" of American society, eventually it gets to you. You begin to dehumanize the people you interact with. The "us versus them" mentality comes into play.

This was exactly what happened to one of my West Point classmates. He wanted to become an FBI agent; but was not accepted, so he decided to become a police officer at a local city department because he had always wanted to become a cop. After about four years as a police officer, he decided to quit law enforcement and work in the corporate business sector. When he reflected on his time as a police officer, he told me that he was proud that he served and learned a lot from being a cop, but as time went on, he began to really hate his job. He said he was tired of dealing with the "dregs of society" (the criminals). He said after a while he started to really dislike dealing with all this "low life." When he began developing an unhealthy attitude that was affecting his physical and mental well-being, he knew it was time to quit. To this day, he is happy that he changed careers.

This is a recurring theme among many law enforcement officers. After years of service and dealing with criminals in sinister environments, some police begin view these people as evil or dirty, thereby shifting their own moral compass. Soldiers have similar experiences, and it can be much worse than law enforcement during war and combat. As the soldiers are thrusted into a world of death and violence, they get desensitized and can become the very evil that they despise. When that happens, they can yearn to kill these "dehumanized enemies" in foreign countries.

Beyond law enforcement, the FBI is also tasked with counterintelligence, where the moral standards sink even lower. In the world of espionage, it is all smoke and mirrors, and the deceit and lies can get so overwhelming that a person or even an organization can be paralyzed with the paranoia of not knowing who to trust or what is true. It is easy for the leaders of an organization to lose their moral compass. The answer to this dilemma is *strong* leadership. Organizations with strong leaders can ride through the dark storms where the visibility is lost because the captain of the ship will always ensure that God and country are his north star. Due to lack of strong leadership, the US government has immorally and unconstitutionally overstepped its mark; the government has lost its trust with the American people.

Upon graduating from the academy and being sent out to the field, it became even more clear that a career in the FBI was probably not a good fit for me. Having worked on joint cases with the other alphabet soup agencies, I also realized that this "deficit of leadership" disease was rampant throughout the government. The culture of the **bureaucratic-socialist-government sector** compared with the **free-market-capitalist-private sector** breeds a different kind of person— one that is risk-adverse and lacking independent thought. The only reason why the military is sometimes immune to this bureaucratic disease is because of war. War is the great crucible of leadership that forces commanders to either succeed in victory or die in defeat. Nature is a very cruel animal. Its bite lasts forever, and forever is exactly how long the leadership lessons will last. One of many problems that I found in the FBI, and in the government in general, was a lack of risk taking with regards to the mission. There is a persistent culture of sheer laziness combined with a culture that is gun-shy toward taking risky chances. As a senior FBI agent once told me:

> David, we can take a big chance on a risky operation, and if we
> succeed, all we are going to get is an attaboy from management,

that's it; however, if we fail, then our career may be over. You
still don't understand the bureau. The aggressive agents get in
trouble; the passive ones get promoted.

Despite only working for three years in the bureau, I had
accomplished more in that time period than most FBI agents or other
US intelligence officers achieve during their entire career lifetimes. The
main reason is because of my willingness to take risks, even if that
meant jeopardizing my own career by breaking rules. I never viewed
breaking regulations as being so serious; however, one must not break
their moral code as that is dishonorable. While in the military, as long
as I put my men and mission first, then I could morally cope with the
consequences of whatever rules I broke.

During my military time both as a cadet and as an officer, I was
brought up on disciplinary charges on numerous occasions. In fact,
one time I almost got a summary court martial. Rumor has it that
soldiers are still talking about my disobedient actions during my time
at the US Army Officer Basic Course (OBC). While attending OBC, I
had threatened to knock out one of my instructors there, who
happened to be a superior officer. Occasional rule breaking is a good
sign of leadership. The key determining factor is whether the offense
was done with moral or immoral intent.

Leaders are less interested in following the rules just for the sake
of following rules. They are more interested in doing what is morally
right and getting the job done. They have a strong sense of loyalty to
their people and to God. While in the Army, I always made sure to
take care of my soldiers, because as a leader you are only as strong as
your team; without the support of your followers, you as a leader will

fail. During my entire time in the Army; I had never forgotten the two essential ingredients for leadership success:

Mission First
People Always

Regarding one of my cases in the FBI, I purposely and secretly broke FBI regulations by circumventing the rules to gain privileged access on a foreign target. The legal and standard route of obtaining information on this person was taking too long. I was afraid I would miss the window of opportunity before this person departed the country, so I took the risky initiative. The FBI never knew what I did, and my operation proved so successful I eventually gained privileged access to a tier one sensitive target. Initially, my bosses were extremely excited about the intelligence penetration and thus supervised my operation intently and with anticipation. As the operation progressed, management began to worry about the sensitive international implications of the operation. They were worried about their own job security and career advancement. This target was so sensitive and valuable that an intelligence officer can rise through the ranks of his entire career just by handling this one asset alone and nothing else. As my operation continued to progress, my managers suddenly called me into the office and told me the operation was getting too sensitive. Due to the international political scope of the operation, they recommended (ordered me) to cease the operation and allow the target to leave the country. I was stunned. I could not believe how timid they were.

One of the main problems with American government leaders, and especially with the FBI, is that there are just too many lawyers in charge who don't understand both leadership and national security. There is too much of a "red-tape, inflexible, administrative lawyer type" culture. There is a serious lack of leadership throughout the US Government and all its departments. In one case, I was working jointly with a CIA officer. She was a nice person, and we got along well enough; however, I was not impressed with her to say the least. She didn't know much about the target country and had minimal foreign language skills. She made it clear to me on numerous occasions that she was a "strong woman"; I made it clear to her on numerous occasions that men are stronger. I am sure she was the typical product of government-sponsored affirmative action initiatives in order to bring in a more "diverse" talent pool to the already mediocre government line up protecting America's national security.

One would think that those individuals who choose to work in national security, would be the highest-level risk takers in the country; however, this is certainly not the case as most people working in the government are risk adverse. The real risk takers of America are the true backbone of America. They are the small business entrepreneurs who have risked their savings in pursuit of their vision and dream. This was my father, who became an entrepreneur at the age of twenty-five. I witnessed my father struggle through the ups and downs of running his business. The daily stress that entrepreneurs go through is enough to make most people reluctant to ever contemplate even starting a business in the first place. Whereas the government employee has a guaranteed monthly paycheck with all the medical, pension, and other benefits that go along with it. The entrepreneur, on the other hand, will sometimes wonder if he will earn enough income in a month to be able to feed his family. If the entrepreneur does not succeed in his mission, it could literally mean the end for him and his family. Most people have no idea the amount of pressure and uphill battles that small business entrepreneurs must go through on a routine basis. For example, my father had told me a story of a major business setback that occurred to him when he was starting out his new tree business in Westchester, New York back in the 1970s. He had just spent ten thousand US dollars of his own money to purchase a new industrial wood chipper. A few days later, someone broke into his parking lot and stole the wood chipper. My father bootstrapped his entire business, so every dollar counted toward his personal investment into the business. Having his wood chipper stolen was no small financial setback; however he spent another ten thousand US dollars and purchased another wood chipper only to discover a few weeks later that this wood chipper was yet again stolen. The amount of violent rage and hostile anger erupting from my father was so intense that my father would later tell me, "David, when my second wood chipper was stolen, I was so angry that if I found out who stole my chipper I would have shot him dead in cold blood." To most Americans, my father's death threat may be perceived as crazy. However, as most people who have never been small business entrepreneurs themselves, they probably will never understand the mindset and stress of an entrepreneur.

The Land of the Free and the Home of the Brave

During my second year at the FBI, the friction between me and the management increased dramatically due to an unexpected and bizarre incident. A foreign intelligence penetration occurred resulting in what I firmly believed to be a strategic advantage to the United States (and later in life, this was confirmed to be true). FBI Management, however, perceived it as an insider threat, a national security breach. Without going into all the details of what happened, the gist of the story is that I became acquainted with a young Chinese woman who was studying for a graduate degree in America. We had met through some Chinese educational seminars. I had never told her my true identity, nor did we ever discuss topics relating to government or national security. On one occasion, she invited me back to her house (in the US). During my visit with her, she told me that she was living with her parents who also had moved to America from China. I asked her what her parents did for work, and she informed me that they worked in the Chinese Consulate. I immediately became both interested and alarmed. I asked her if she could show me pictures of her parents. She did, and I confirmed her parents' Chinese names. When I left her house, I immediately drove to the FBI field office and conducted a query, which did not take me long at all. The parents where suspected Chinese intelligence officers from the Ministry of State Security (MSS). They were posing as diplomats assigned to one of the Chinese Consulates in the United States. As soon as I discovered this information, I realized that I stumbled onto something very serious. I called my FBI mentor. He was my Yoda; he had a true fondness for West Pointers and kept reminding me why military men sometimes make bad intelligence officers, even though he had a deep admiration for the military. He always kept telling me that I needed to abandon my military behavior and adapt it to intelligence. He kept saying: "You military guys are too much hard chargers; you're always taking the fight directly to the enemy. You got to be like the Vietcong: sneaky, indirect, ambiguous."

When I told him what happened, he was shocked. He told me to immediately break off contact with the Chinese woman and never tell the FBI about what happened—to just forever keep it a secret and move on. He warned me that the FBI has no qualms with burning their own; they are ultimately bureaucrats, and that FBI management will always protect themselves over the field agents. I reasoned with him that my visit should not be viewed negatively. On the contrary, this was a great opportunity for the bureau to exploit this once in a lifetime intelligence penetration. I told him, I already have access to the house and daughter. I could easily gain access to the parents and more. This is a huge opportunity for the bureau to go on the offensive. His demeanor changed. With both concern and trepidation in his voice he said, "David be very careful; I am worried about you. Management will destroy you and never even think twice about it. Just walk away from this and never breathe a word about it. If you tell them FBI management will look upon you as a threat; they will not trust you, so do not trust them.

Looking back, I should have listened to Yoda; through his decades of running intelligence operations in the bureau, he knew how FBI Management would react, and he was right. Instead, I decided to tell my FBI supervisor what had happened. My supervisor was in complete shock, and in a matter of minutes, I was on the top floor standing at attention at the desk of the FBI Assistant Special Agent in Charge of

Counterintelligence in what turned out to be both an unprofessional and unpleasant exchange. First, she was very interested in hearing about my sexual relations with the Chinese woman and made some distasteful remarks regarding the subject. She interrogated me and then ended the meeting by ordering me to fly to headquarters for a security debriefing immediately. I asked her why I was being punished as I had not done anything wrong. She was a fake feminist, so we didn't get along very well. In addition, unbeknownst to me, FBI management immediately launched a secret internal national security investigation against me. They began spying on me behind on my back, making up absolutely ridiculous charges of espionage, which included among other things the country of Israel.

The management removed me from all intelligence work and assigned me to administrative duties. After around six months of negative treatment, I finally submitted my paperwork for resignation. FBI management was happy to see me leave, and I was happy to be leaving. Before I could leave the FBI, however, I was approached by a team of undercover FBI agents who were secretly conducting the investigation on me—basically spying on me behind my back. They had finally approached me overtly. They wanted to interrogate me, which I voluntarily agreed to even though I did not need to cooperate with them since I was quitting the FBI anyway.

The interrogation revealed the length of their covert investigation against me. Finally, the agents asked me if I was willing to take a polygraph test before I leave the FBI. I could have easily said no; however, to uphold my family name and that of West Point, I volunteered to take it. They basically wanted to know if I was a spy, a mole within the FBI. The polygraph examiner flew in all the way from headquarters. I was put in an isolated room. As I sat in the chair with the wires and straps all around me I kept thinking how immoral and incompetent the FBI is. After the polygraph was complete, the examiner told me the official results, declaring that he witnessed no signs of deception. I told him of course not; I did not spy on my country, nor did I ever intend to. I then shook my head in disgust at the entire clown show.

Back at my desk, I threw my badge, gun, and key card in my drawer and texted the FBI secretary, saying goodbye, I am now leaving, and will see myself out the door. When I finally left the federal building, I breathed a sigh of relief and was happy at the thought of starting the next new chapter of my life, which was pursuing a master's in public policy from Harvard University. Yes, it's an overrated degree at a pretentious university; however, I was just glad to be out of the spy business and looked forward to beginning a new career in the private sector.

That night I headed to the airport with luggage in tow ready to fly to Boston to begin the Harvard program. As I was checking in at the ticket counter, suddenly three FBI agents approached me with guns on their sides. They ordered me to come talk with them; I told them, "I am not interested. I am no longer in the FBI. Goodbye." They closed in on me in a threatening manner and ordered me to follow them into a secluded room in the airport. I realized something serious was afoot and immediately became defensive. "No way! I am not interested. Please go away," I told them.

They would not leave me alone. I was now in the airport terminal hallway with my back to the wall while these three FBI agents physically blocked my escape. I was literally a captive audience. "What do you want?" I asked. The senior agent began interrogating me yet again, accusing me of being a spy. The whole scene was so ridiculous and unprofessional. I told him that I had already answered all the questions from the FBI Internal Investigation Team. I told them that I had never committed espionage, nor did I have any intention of ever committing espionage. Still, they continued to unlawfully detain me. I told them they were going to make me miss my flight and that I was not interested in talking with them anymore and to stop detaining me. Finally, the senior agent pulled out a multiple-page document, handed me a pen, and told me to sign it.

"What's this," I asked him. He said it was my out-processing paperwork; I told him I was not interested in signing anything.

He pushed the pen in my hands and yelled, "SIGN IT!"

By this time the whole situation was tense and hostile. I was being detained against my will. I was being ordered to sign something that I did not want to sign nor even had the chance to read or understand. This is how Third-World countries treat their citizens. I involuntarily signed the paperwork and then asked him if I was free to go. He looked at me in total disgust, and said, "Go."

When I was about to board the airplane, the airline employee told me that my luggage was selected for secondary screening, so I needed to accompany them to witness my bags being thoroughly inspected. When I finally arrived at Harvard, I put an account of my FBI experiences and the immoral treatment at the hands of the FBI management in a letter to Senator Chuck Grassley.

My decision to leave the bureau was quite rare. Despite all the trouble I got into, I could have continued to work there. Albeit, I probably would have permanently been assigned to the administration squad, doing menial case work and would have never been promoted. It is almost impossible to terminate an FBI agent. I could tell from the very beginning that the culture of the FBI was not the right fit for me.

One thing that really left an impression upon me was the level of arrogance and ego. In the military, the Army guys would often make fun of the Navy SEALs for being the most egotistical and flamboyant members of the military. I personally have always admired the Army Special Forces (Green Berets), who are known as the "quiet professionals." The SEALs extravagant ego pales in comparison to the FBI's. The FBI has the most elevated sense of importance than any other US government agency; their ego is enormous. The FBI relishes in the fact that they are the highest-level law enforcement and national security entity in the country; their legal authority grants them the power to arrest anyone in the nation, whether it is the CIA, military, NSA, State Department, Congress, judges, and even the President of the United States. This authority gives them a sense of an unmistakable amount of power, and an ego the size of their budget. Their power is felt in the way these agents walk, talk, and act; they exude ego. The culture of the FBI is one of power and secrets.

After I left the FBI, and even after I left America, the FBI has continued to spy on me and damage my life and reputation. Since the FBI doesn't have any evidence against me, they have thus focused on my conversative political views as justification to continue to spy on me and damage my life. For example, during my last visit to the United States, I was detained, interrogated, searched, humiliated, surveilled, deceived, and assaulted by FBI and DHS agents. After that incident, I arranged a meeting with FBI management at the US embassy in Beijing, China. During our face-the-face meeting, I informed them that I was fully aware that they were investigating me. I requested that they confront me in person and formally state their allegations to my face. The FBI ignored my requests, leaving me with few options to remedy this violation of my constitutional rights. I escalated my grievance to the inspector general of the Department of Justice (Michael E. Horowitz). He too ignored me. I also petitioned US Senators and US Congressmen to help with my cause; they also ignored me. Therefore, I have decided to go public with my complaint against the FBI. This is not just my fight; this fight is for the constitutional rights of all American citizens, to protect them from the tyrannical American government and specifically from the increasingly corrupt and immoral management of the FBI. If the FBI can so easily trample upon my constitutional rights, then all Americans are vulnerable to their power and wrath.

Leadership
Is the Invitation to Judgement

The whistleblower system in America is broken in both the US government and US corporations—as I will detail later in the book about the unethical behavior of my former employers who all took retaliatory action against me for being an ethical whistleblower (Boeing, Amazon, Kimberly Clark, and GEODIS).

When a whistleblower exposes unethical misconduct, either nothing changes and/or the whistleblower is punished. When the system is broken, the leader needs to take charge.

Two examples of courageous whistleblowers who took charge are Edward Snowden and Julian Assange. Both men are patriotic heroes. When I exposed the FBI's unethical investigation against me, they ignored me, the inspector general of the Department of Justice ignored me, and finally the US politicians ignored me.

The whistleblower system is utterly broken and thus my only option left is to take my fight to the American public. This book is ultimately an omen of the future of American leadership and of a major collapse or civil war. Within the leadership void of America sooner or later patriotic Americans will take a stand and defend what our American Revolutionary forefathers fought and died for: **Faith, Family,** and **Freedom**. As the decline of America continues, more and more Americans will come to the realization that a great leadership evolution is underway in America. May God bless the patriots and may the patriots have no fear.

> **Be strong and courageous. Do not be afraid or terrified because of them, for the LORD your God goes with you; he will never leave you nor forsake you.**
> **(Deuteronomy 31:6 NIV)**

4

Request for Government Oversight

Despite my repeated requests, the FBI was unwilling to communicate with me because, as I have stated, there is no evidence against me. The FBI's investigation against me is due to my strong conservative political values. Therefore, I was left with no other choice but to submit a formal written complaint to the inspector generals of the United Stated Departments of Justice (DOJ) and Homeland Security (DHS)—as well as to all US Senators and Congressmen—on 4 January 2022. I specifically called upon senators Chuck Grassley, Ted Cruz, Rand Paul, and Tom Cotton for assistance. For over a year I petitioned every single US politician asking for their help; however, nobody responded to my letter or my monthly email reminders, not one single congressman or senator. It is so ridiculous and hypocritical when these same politicians talk about how thankful they are towards military veterans; shear propaganda. It just shows that not only is the whistleblower system in America truly broken, but our country in general is truly broken. Below is an edited paraphrase of the complaint I sent to the US government. The full-length complaints can be accessed on my website (www.terebinth.info).

––––––––

Complaint #1, against the Department of Homeland Security Customs and Border Protection

RE: Civil rights and civil liberties issue of abusive or coercive questioning and unreasonable searches and seizures upon entry into the USA via Chicago O'Hare International Airport.

During my encounter with the CBP officers on 18 August 2019 at the Chicago O'Hare International Airport, the officers interrogating me used abusive or coercive questioning and unreasonable searches and seizures. During my initial encounter with the officers, I instructed them that I do not consent to any questions or searches unless mandated by law. Despite my stated instruction, the officers continued to ask me questions and were perplexed as to why I was not willing to talk. Their coercive questioning included:

Why don't you want to tell us? These are just simple questions. You don't know where you are staying? We just want to know. Why won't you answer the question? You don't think it is odd; that you don't want to answer these questions?

Another key point is that during the secondary inspection, as I was instructed to report to the CBP desk, there were two CBP officers behind an elevated desk/counter. I began to record my interaction with the officers using my mobile phone, and they immediately ordered me to stop recording. The CBP officer directly in front of me extended his arm with open hand to block the phone camera and again ordered me to stop filming. At that time, I complied with the order and stopped filming.

Are U.S. Citizens allowed to record (via their personal mobile device, for example) CBP inspections insides US airports where the search is specifically being targeted against the US citizen who desires to record the event? I would like a clear answer on this.

I wanted to record the secondary inspection being conducted on me. I was specifically ordered by the CBP officer at the desk that I was NOT allowed to make any recordings with my mobile phone. Is it against the law to record CBD officers?

In the report you have provided me (Exhibit Number Two) there is no mention of the search of my mobile phone, which I did not consent to. The CBP officer instructed me to unlock my phone and surrender it for inspection. Then my phone was taken into a secluded room where I was not allowed to be present. I waited for over an hour until my phone was returned to me. Why is there no account of this in the CBP records you have provided me (Exhibit Number Two)? In addition, why was my phone searched at all? What did the CBP agents do to my mobile phone? Was it manipulated in any way? Was any data or applications removed or added to my mobile phone? Was my mobile phone returned to me in the "same exact" condition as to the time when I involuntarily surrendered my phone to the CBP Officer? Was my mobile phone manipulated, altered, or changed in any way by the CBP officers or another agency when my phone was in their possession?

———————

Complaint #2, against the CBP

RE: Civil rights and civil liberties issue of abusive or coercive questioning and unreasonable searches and seizures during exit from the USA via Chicago O'Hare International Airport.

During my encounter with two CBP officers on 22 August 2019 at the Chicago O'Hare International Airport, the officers interrogating me used "abusive or coercive questioning and unreasonable searches and seizures." During my initial encounter with the officers, I instructed both of them that I do not consent to any questions or searches unless mandated by law. Despite my stated instruction, the officers continued to intimidate me.

Exhibit Number One attached to this email states "Personal Search: NO." If this is indicating that no personal searches were conducted by the two officers, then this statement is false. Allow me to illustrate just how invasive and humiliating this detainment, which was conducted in plain sight of fellow passengers, airline, and airport employees, was:

1. I was instructed to sit on the ground for approximately twenty minutes crossed legged as the contents of my backpack were pulled out and placed on the ground in front of me. The CPB officers inventoried every single item and then asked me questions about these items, which I again, never consented to and reminded them that I didn't consent to any questions.

2. While sitting on the ground, I was ordered to take off my shoes and ordered to remove the soles of the shoes. Afterward my shoes were thoroughly inspected by the officers.

3. My fanny pack's contents were emptied on the ground (for the public to see) by the two officers, who then searched and inventoried all the contents, interrogating me over every item.

4. When I finally was able to stand up, I was subjected to a full body search; this included an officer groping my groin area. I received a full pat down as one would get when one is arrested—all in plain view of fellow passengers. It was completely humiliating, especially as a military veteran and a US citizen. Why was I singled out and not the other passengers who were not US citizens? I asked them. They did not provide me with any answers. They just wanted to know why I was not cooperating with them as they continued to interrogate me against my will.

To further illustrate just how invasive this search was, the officers searched through an orange notebook of mine; they photographed all the information contained in the notebook, including what appeared to be telephone numbers, which they asked me to whom they belonged; when I replied (repeatedly) that I do not consent to any questioning, one of the officers replied, "Don't worry, I can find out right now; why don't I just call them," while making a move for his mobile phone. I told him he was acting unprofessional and that this treatment was uncalled for!

Exhibit Number One, the report written about my testimony, is both false and taken out of context. Regarding the interrogation I received, below is some of the officers unreasonable line of questioning despite me formally telling both of them that I do not consent to any questioning:

1. "Just tell us where you were staying in Chicago. Just give us some hints; I need some information to write in my report."

2. "If you do not cooperate with us, you will miss your flight."

3. "If you do not answer our questions, then I will get my supervisor involved, and you can talk with him."

4. After I unwillingly told the officers my reason for traveling to Thailand, one officer replied, "OK, now tell us the real reason why you are going to Thailand."

5. "You better tell us everything; we are going to find out anyway."

6. As the officers were counting my money, they asked me, "What do you do for work?" and "How much money do you make?" When I refused to answer the questions, they said, "What are you hiding? Just tell us what do you do for work; it is a simple question."

7. As the officers realized that I did not want to cooperate with them, one officer threatened me by saying, "I can escalate this matter if you want; I don't think you want that."

The interrogation took so long that the flight attendant, who was standing at the open door on the boarding ramp into the airplane and had direct line of sight during my entire detainment, motioned to the CPB officers to indicate that the plane needed to depart. As soon as I was released, I immediately boarded the airplane, and the Stewardess standing at the open door directly ushered me to my seat. The entire plane had been waiting on me. The passengers knew that I was the reason the flight was being delayed and were staring at me as I walked the aisle to my seat. Rows and rows of these passengers who had previously witnessed me being searched and interrogated like a criminal stared at me. It was very humiliating. They had witnessed the CBP Officers searching both my belongings and my person. They had a look of apprehension as I boarded the plane, as if a wanted criminal just stepped on board and their safety was now threatened with my presence. As soon as I was seated, the plane immediately pulled away from the gate.

Complaint #3, against the Department of Justice Federal Bureau of Investigation

RE: Spying on a US citizen

I am fully aware of the FBI's unethical and unconstitutional investigation against me, which includes but is not limited to the following:

1. The unwanted solicitation of my friends, contacts, colleagues, associates, and family to acquire confidential information about me.

2. The unwanted solicitation of these above individuals to act as a paid agents on behalf of the FBI for them to surreptitiously gain confidential information about me.

————————

Compliant #4, against the Department of Justice Federal Bureau of Investigation

RE: Assault, stalking, and lying to a US citizen

At approximately noon on 20 August 2019, I was located in the city of Chicago in Grant Park by myself. I noticed a man stalking me. The description of this man is below:

> White, Caucasian Male
> Approximately 33 years old
> Approximately 5 foot 9 inches tall
> Approximately 165lbs
> Clean shaven and short cropped brown hair
> Short-sleeved, collared blueish gray shirt and khaki shorts

I noticed the man following me around in the park for approximately one hour. His actions made me feel very uncomfortable and threatened; he was stalking me. Everywhere I walked, this man would continue to stalk me, observing my every movement. While at a water fountain area, when this man was approximately thirty meters away, I finally decided to run away. I sprinted about 150 meters, quickly turning through the various corners in the park and eventually ending up at the end of a corner path, an L-shaped road in the back of the park. I abruptly stopped and turned around to observe this same man running in full pursuit. As the man turned the corner in a full run, he stopped dead in his tracks when he spotted me about twenty meters away. I glared directly into his eyes, and he looked at me in shock. He had been uncovered; his secret stalking operation against me had been revealed.

He then slowly walked directly toward me, catching his breath. I continued to face this man with my eyes focused on him. He approached me in a threatening manner. That was the first time I had ever seen this man in my life; he was an absolute stranger to me, stalking me. At that time, however, I was completely convinced that he was an FBI agent or an FBI surveillance operative. I knew if this man would physically attack me, I would be legally obstructed from defending myself due to this man's federal law enforcement status. I was afraid I would be charged with assaulting a federal officer; I was thus frightened, remained still, and prayed for my safety.

He was huffing and puffing, visibly angered and walking directly toward me with his hands opening and closing into fists. I was standing still in fear; not sure whether to run away or stand my ground. As he approached closer, I could see in his eyes that he was angry he had been discovered stalking me; his sinister secret had been revealed. As he walked closer and closer to me, my fear heightened as to what this man planned to do with me, *What are his motives? Why is he still pursuing me, and now directly walking right up to me in a threatening manner?*

As he walked up to me, he began assuming a fighting posture with his hands balled up into fists. As he was within two meters of me, continuing to walk toward me in a threatening manner— no words from either of us had thus been said—I could tell this man was furious; his facial features showed signs that a physical confrontation was about to happen. It was an extremely tense moment. Trying to deescalate the hostile situation, I kept my left arm down by my side, I extended out my right hand in the manner to shake someone's hand in a normal greeting. As the man approached, he grabbed my right hand; it was an exaggerated grip, attempting to squeeze and crush my hand. As he grabbed my hand; I immediately asked him:

"Are you following me?"

"No!"

When I asked him this question, he became even more infuriated. Because he knew that his answer was a lie, he replied to me in a harsh "No!" as if that was the most ridiculous question he had ever heard. His eyes were fixed to mine in a deadly stare down. This man's actions and behavior at this time; made me feel that he was an absolute threat to my life and safety.

"You wouldn't lie to me, would you?" I asked.

"No!!!" he said.

After I asked him this second question, his response of "No!" was harsh and angry. He obviously was aware of the fact that I knew he was lying to me. He then forcibly rotated my arm toward my stomach. My elbow was still bent, however, my right hand was now pushed into my body. As the man did this, he stepped closer to me in a violent manner. He violently pivoted his body and struck me in my stomach with his elbow and my chest with his shoulder. I was completely taken off guard as I had refrained from making any posture or movements that would indicate I was prepared to fight this man. The force from this man was so strong, I was immediately spun around like getting hit by a boxer conducting a violent right hook. After he hit me with these two blows, we released our grip and I rotated both backward and counterclockwise. We were now positioned approximately 180 degrees from our original position to each other. He had to turn slightly to face me, regaining his footing and posture after the torquing motion of his boxing-like right hook he had just given me. I was having trouble breathing as the man's first attack (the elbow blow) hit me in my solar plexus. I could feel the shock and pain in both my solar plexus (his right elbow attack) and also my chest (his right shoulder attack). I was in a complete state of shock and terror. My mind was racing. I knew I could not call the police nor physically defend myself from this man because he was part of federal law enforcement; I was in absolute disbelief at what had just occurred.

Following the assault, we were standing about two meters apart and roughly 180 degrees different from when we first encountered. I am in shock, and my defenses are ready for a full-on confrontation. I was in fight or flight mode. Since I was convinced I would be arrested if I fought back, retreating and escaping was my only option. The man continued to stare at me in anger, furious, and breathing heavily but not saying a word. The situation was completely surreal. *Who is this man? Why is he stalking me? Why did he just assault me? What is he going to do to me next?* These questions raced in my mind as the two of us continued to stare down one another.

For a full five to ten seconds we stared each other down; his hands were clenched, and he was visibly shaking in anger. As I braced myself for another physical altercation with this man, I summoned my military command voice and directly shouted at him: "Stop following me!" I then immediately turned around and began to run. I ran away and did not look back. After running for about 150 meters, I decided to exit the park and cross South Michigan Avenue. As I looked behind me, I saw this same man pursuing me; this time, however, he seemed to be shouting in what appeared to be his mobile phone, as if giving a report to someone about my movement and direction while watching my every movement. As the man continued to get closer to me, I crossed the dangerous avenue even though the crosswalk light was red and there was moving traffic. I was frightened by this man who continued to stalk me and had already assaulted me. I ran across the street, putting myself in a dangerous situation as I had to dodge the oncoming cars. I then proceeded to run away without looking back. I entered various buildings and continued to perform escape and evade movements until I did not see that man again. Upon finding a safe and secluded place to regain my composure, I was in complete shock and fear. I succinctly remember at that very moment, *My own government is hunting me!*. As I caught my breath and collected myself, my survival instincts began to take charge.

———————

Compliant #5, against the FBI

RE: Unethical failure to communicate with me.

Knowing full well the FBI has an ongoing investigation on me in autumn 2019, I reached out to the FBI legal attaché stationed at the US embassy in Beijing, China. Around November 2019 I received an email from SXXX. SXXX informed me that he was the newly assigned FBI legal attaché to the US embassy in Beijing, China, and that he was willing to meet and talk with me. In January 2020, I met with both SXXX and his deputy in a cafe in Beijing. SXXX's deputy was DXXX, the FBI assistant legal attaché assigned to the US embassy in Beijing, China. I informed SXXX and DXXX what the purpose of this meeting was and that I had three specific points to formally communicate with them.

The first point was that I was fully aware that I was under investigation by the FBI, I specifically recalled the accounts of my previous detainments, interrogations, and searches on the part of the CBP during my entry and exit at the Chicago O'Hare International Airport. I also informed SXXX and DXXX that during my time in Chicago I was under surveillance by the FBI and had had a physical confrontation with either an FBI agent or an FBI surveillance operative. I furthermore stated that the FBI has been soliciting my family, friends, contacts, and associates for information about me and get them to work as paid agents on behalf of the FBI. I informed them of the tremendous damage to my reputation and integrity the FBI has done by surreptitiously conducting this investigation behind my back.

The second point was for SXXX to formally communicate to FBI HQ that I was fully aware of this investigation against me and to immediately cease and desist this unlawful and groundless investigation behind my back.

The third point was for the FBI to immediately arrange a face-to-face meeting with me and formally declare what their allegation is against me in relation to their investigation—to have the courage and integrity to face me; and level the allegation(s) to my face.

SXXX said that he was not aware of any of the information that I had presented to him. He told me he would inform FBI HQ and see what they say; he also said he will enquire about my CBP incident in Chicago.

Below are some of the email correspondences between SXXX and me. As you can see, the FBI HQ has been formally informed and that I have requested to speak with them about their unethical investigation into me and yet they still have not responded to me; however, they continue with their spy operation targeted against me.

From: David Baumblatt
<leadership@terebinth.info>

Sent: Friday, April 3, 2020 6:40 PM

To: SXXX (Beijing) <SXXX@state.gov>; DXXX (Beijing)
<DXXX@state.gov>

Subject: Meeting

Thanks SXXX,

I can confirm that, yes, harassment and racism have been increasing here in China just as nationalism has increased; however, especially with the recent virus outbreak, it is just not a safe place to be any more if you are a foreigner; however, especially if you are an American. I believe it will get worse.

Yes, I would appreciate it if you can get feedback regarding the incident at the Chicago O'Hare airport; that was the same airport I flew in and out of, and I was checked in secondary both flying into and out of the airport. Again, I found it down right embarrassing and unpatriotic that I was searched in that manner, even with all my stuff on the ground (during the exit check having to sit on the ground, my phone was taken from me, my personal clothing I was wearing searched, and I was interrogated, yes interrogated, as I repeatedly said, I wished to make no comments to the officers); I do not think they realize just how disrespectful and unpatriotic their actions were to treat a military veteran that way; all the while Chinese nationals walked freely by me; free to go as they please in and out of America, doing who knows what.

Thanks

David

~~~~~~~~~

From: SXXX (Beijing) <SXXX@state.gov>

Sent: Friday, April 3, 2020 1:00 PM

To: David Baumblatt <leadership@terebinth.info>; DXXX (Beijing) <DXXX@state.gov>

Subject: Meeting

Hi David,

I am sorry for our slow response back. I have been out of the office for the last couple of days. The COVID-19 outbreak has consumed all my attention lately. The entire office has been evacuated and I am the only one that remains. Hopefully you have stayed healthy during these past two months and that no one you know in the U.S. has been negatively impacted by the virus. If you can share, I would be curious to know if as an expat living in China during this episode if you have experienced any uptick in harassment from the Chinese over the COVID-19 rhetoric. I am trying to track that information.

With that said, we were not able to find out anything from FBI HQ about you being a subject or not. We were able to confirm that you had been an employee but that wasn't ever really in doubt. I did reach out to a CBP contact to try and determine if he could confirm whether you underwent secondary screening during your last trip to the U.S. However, I have not heard back yet and honestly that does not surprise me given what has happened here with the evacuations and all. Therefore, I will reach out to him again now and see if I can get you some information sooner rather than later.

Monday is a holiday and the embassy is closed but if I hear anything back in the next couple of days from CBP then I will let you know as soon as possible.

SXXX

———————

Compliant #6, against the FBI

RE: Disclosure of a US citizen's private confidential information to a foreign government(s).

Has the FBI, or any other US agency, or US official, communicated with a foreign government, foreign governmental department, or foreign government official where the subject of the communication was me?

I am a private US citizen, and my private matters are confidential; they are classified. For the US government to communicate behind my back to foreign governments about me is traitorous. If the US government sees no fault in this matter, or does not even understand why a private American citizen would be outraged by this treacherous act, then what if the opposite situation would occur:

1. The US government communicates with a foreign government about the confidential/classified matters of a private US citizen.

2. A private US citizen communicates with a foreign government about the confidential/classified matters of the US government.

––––––––

As a reminder, the full twenty-seven-page complaint can be found on my website (www.terebinth.info). Also the entire email chain to FBI management, the inspector generals of the DOJ and DHS, as well to all the US Congressman and Senators, spanning over one year, can also be shared.

Reducing the Tyranny of FISA

One concrete step in reducing the tyrannical powers of the government, and particularly with the FBI, is to reform the Foreign Intelligence Surveillance Act (FISA). The FISA is a federal law that establishes the procedures for the surveillance and collection of foreign intelligence. It requires federal law enforcement and intelligence agencies to obtain authorization for gathering "foreign intelligence information" between "foreign powers" and "agents of foreign powers" suspected of espionage or terrorism. The law established the Foreign Intelligence Surveillance Court (FISC) to oversee requests for surveillance warrants. Although FISA was initially limited to government use of electronic surveillance, subsequent amendments have broadened the law to regulate other intelligence-gathering methods, including physical searches, pen register and trap and trace devices, devices, and compelling the production of certain types of business records. Approval of a FISA application requires the court to find probable cause that the target of the surveillance be a "foreign power" or an "agent of a foreign power" inside the United States and that the places at which surveillance is requested is used or will be used by that foreign power or its agent. The (FISC) is located in Washington, DC, and is staffed by eleven judges appointed by the Chief Justice of the United States. The court hears evidence presented solely by the Department of Justice. There is no provision for a release of information regarding such hearings, or for the record of information actually collected. FISC meets in secret and approves or denies requests for search warrants. In addition to electronic surveillance, FISA permits the physical search of the "premises, information, material, or property used exclusively by" a foreign power. The requirements and procedures are nearly identical to those for electronic surveillance.

I am in full support with FISA as it is applied to foreign nationals. During my time in the FBI, I had no guilt or qualms with using FISA to spy on foreign nationals. Regarding its use against US Citizens however, FISA should be abolished. The problem rests with its use against US citizens in violation to the Fourth Amendment, which is quite clear in protecting the privacy rights of American citizens. The Fourth Amendment was written to keep the government out of our private affairs and off our backs. It requires probable cause — evidence that (a) a crime was committed and (b) it is likely that execution of the warrant will produce more evidence of that crime. The Fourth Amendment explicitly outlaws general warrants that permit the bearer to search wherever he wishes and seize whatever he finds. The amendment requires every warrant to describe specifically the place to be searched or the person or thing to be seized. We cannot continue to provide our government with clandestine spying powers that violate the Fourth Amendment rights of Americans.

When governments spy on their own citizens, the decline of trust will lead to the decline of freedom.

5

Patriotism: We Lead through the Blood of Our Nation

What is an American patriot? This question can easily be altered to read: What is a Chinese, British, German, Israeli, Indian, Mexican patriot? The nationality may change, but the meaning of the word *patriot* does not. The word *patriot* is derived from the Greek word *patrios*, meaning "of one's father." To be a patriot you must love your father and more important love your fatherland. Hence *patriotism* is the love of your country.

With respect to leadership, what is a country? How can someone actually love a country? Like everything in leadership, it always revolves around people. Just as a patriot loves his father, a patriot must also love his countrymen or his compatriots. The most important element of a country are the people, the citizens. Therefore, to love your country means to love the citizens of your country. Your compatriots, or your fellow citizens, are like your extended family; together you think and feel through the blood of your nation. You live together, thrive together, fight together, and ultimately achieve victory or suffer defeat together. Consider the American Revolution.

Patriots were known as Revolutionaries, Continentals, Rebels, or American Whigs. They were citizens of the thirteen colonies who rejected British rule and declared the United States of America an independent nation in July 1776. Today's American government constantly warns against and admonishes any violent means of protest; however, America never would have been founded unless violent means were not taken by our honorable revolutionary forefathers.

The United States government constantly espouses that violence is not the answer; however, America is at a constant state of war or conflict with other nations—constantly exporting overt and covert military violence overseas. The United States government constantly espouses the international rule of law; however, America is constantly and intentionally violating the international law through illegal wars and other illegal activities. The point is to understand leadership, one must have a good grasp on morality and realize it has so many shades of gray; however, the leader must make out black and white to the best of his or her ability. There is an obvious moral contradiction regarding American's stance on violence and illegal activity; the government denounces this type of activity while at the same time exporting this activity across the globe. Furthermore, this great nation never would have been formed if it was not for our the Founding Fathers use of violence and illegal activity.

Patriotic Americas celebrate the Founding Fathers as a group of brave and honorable men who led the war of independence against the tyrannical Great Britain and crafted the framework for a government of the new nation called the United States. When these fifty-six brave and honorable men signed the Declaration of Independence, they knew full well that they were committing treason against the King of England, and they knew the penalty was death. Despite the risks to their and their families' safety, the reality was that the Founding

Fathers valued freedom for themselves and their posterity so much so that they risked their lives, fortunes, and sacred honor. Signing the Declaration proved to be very costly: five signers were captured by the British and brutally tortured as traitors. Nine fought in the Revolutionary War and died from wounds or hardships. Two lost their sons in the war, and two others had sons captured. At least a dozen of the fifty-six had their homes pillaged and burned. Today, America honors its Founding Fathers, but in reality, these men were all considered traitors by the king of England and would have all have been summarily executed as traitors if caught by the British.

**Because they won, America honors these rebel leaders.
However, if they had lost, Britain would have executed them as rebel traitors.**

During the Revolutionary War, those opposing the patriotic Founding Fathers were the loyalists; these were the American colonialists who remained loyal to the British. Why did some colonialists choose to become patriots while others chose to become loyalists?

Historians have explored the motivations that pulled men to one side or the other. Yale historian Leonard Woods Labaree examined the writings of leading men on each side, searching for how personality shaped their choice. He found some unique characteristics that differentiated the two groups.

Patriots vs Loyalists

Loyalists were older, better established, and more likely to resist innovation than the patriots. Loyalists felt that the Crown was the legitimate government and resistance to it was morally wrong. Patriots felt that morality was on their side because the British government had violated the constitutional rights of Englishmen. Men who were alienated by physical attacks on Royal officials took the loyalist position while those who were offended by heavy-handed British response to actions such as the Boston Tea Party became patriots.

Merchants in the port cities with long-standing financial attachments to Britain were likely to remain loyal to the system. Few patriots were deeply enmeshed in the system. Some Loyalists, according to Labaree, were procrastinators who believed that independence was bound to come someday but wanted to postpone the moment. Patriots, on the other hand, wanted to seize the moment.

Loyalists were cautious and afraid of anarchy or tyranny that might come from mob rule. Patriots made a systematic effort to take a stand against the British government. Finally, Labaree argues that loyalists were pessimists who lacked the patriots' confidence that independence lay ahead. The Sons of Liberty was a loosely organized, clandestine, sometimes violent, political organization active in the thirteen American colonies. It was founded to advance the rights of the colonists and to fight taxation by the British government. Their motto became:

No Taxation without Representation

Regarding taxation, America is the only country in the world that taxes its citizens on their worldwide income. If US citizens are permanently living abroad and 100% of their income is foreign sourced, and they of course already pay taxes to the local foreign government, they are still taxed by the American government. Americans are required to pay US taxes even if they do not live or work in America, and therefore they make no income in or from America. When I was living in China and working for Boeing, I was paid in Chinese Renminbi 人民币.[1] Not only did I have to pay taxes to the Chinese government, but I also had to pay taxes to the US government. In fact, the US government garnished my overseas salary without my consent, and despite my having already paying taxes to the Chinese government.

As a US Citizen and military veteran, I am not welcome in the US; however, the government welcomes (and demands) I pay American taxes.

If I am not welcome in the United States, then my overseas tax revenue should not be welcomed either.

Considering America is the only country in the world that taxes its expats, I challenge the US government to afford its expats the protections of the US Constitution no matter where they are physically located. A case in point would be with the unconstitutional US

Criminal Law Border Search Exception, such as a point of exit or entry as in the Chicago O'Hare International Airport. Searches by US law enforcement of US citizens at the border are absolutely unconstitutional. If the American government is going to impose worldwide taxation on its citizens, then US citizens should also be afforded with worldwide US constitutional protections. Law Enforcement should not be allowed to search US Citizens at these border points unless they have probable cause of a crime in line with the Fourth Amendment of the constitution.

Leadership is a dangerous calling and not for the faint of heart.

Jewish Patriots of the Revolution

The American Revolution did not just encompass a homogenous group of men. There were even Jews who were key members of the patriots. When it came to the Revolution, the majority of American Jews sided with the patriots. It was the first time since their exile from Jerusalem that they could fight for freedom alongside their Christian neighbors as equals. Jews were present at Bunker Hill, Valley Forge, and other battle sites throughout the colonies. Behind the scenes, they provided logistic support by equipping soldiers, shipping supplies, and raising funds. Shipowners such as Isaac Moses of Philadelphia outfitted privateers to harass British ships. The privateers engaged in running the British blockade to provide necessary provisions to the needy Revolutionary forces.

One famous member of the Sons of Liberty was Haym Salomon, a Jewish financier of the Revolutionary cause who had immigrated to New York City from Poland. Through the influence of the patriotic New York Sons of Liberty, Salomon obtained a contract to supply American troops in central New York. When the British took New York, Salomon covertly encouraged the Hessian mercenaries fighting for the British to desert. He was arrested, his property confiscated, and he was sentenced to be hanged; however, he managed to escape and fled penniless to Philadelphia. There he set about exchanging Continentals bills for French and Dutch currencies. For his services, he only took a meager one percent of the fees. The Continental Congress officially named him "Broker to the Office of Finance of the United States," and France named him "Treasurer of the French Army in America."

Salomon also provided interest-free loans to "James Madison, Thomas Jefferson, James Wilson, Edmond Randolph, and Generals von Steuben, St. Clair, and Mifflin of the Continental Army. The diaries of Robert Morris, superintendent of finances, contain several appreciative references to the "little Jew broker." When Salomon died in 1745 at forty-five years old, he was $638,000 in debt to "public and private creditors," with the government never returning the money they owed him.

Leadership rests in the hands of God.

Through victory and defeat, man's morality will be cemented on the battlefield.

During the Civil War, West Point brothers in arms turned against each other and fought on their respective sides of the Union North and Confederate South. They battled each other to the death, and the country was torn apart. America will be headed for this disaster again unless it drastically changes its moral course. For example, in the FBI's illegal spy campaign against me for my political views, they have immorally solicited the help from some of my once-trusted West Point friends and colleagues, enlisting them to surreptitiously gain information about me. These once honorable West Point friends of mine, under the instruction of the FBI, voluntarily acted as paid government agents to spy on me, to dishonor the bonds of loyalty in both friendship and the academy. Just like West Point brothers fought against each other during the Civil War, the military bonds of today's American military veterans are breaking apart. When the hallowed institution of West Point ceases to uphold a sense of honor and trust among its own graduates, then as the long gray line of alumni will break, as graduates lose their trusted bond amongst each other, so too will West Point's trusted bond with America be dissolved. There is nothing more American than West Point, and its hallowed halls and castle walls give Americans a sense of security and trust. There was always the hope and trust that West Point would guide America through to safety during past wars and conflicts, and the country would always be secure because of the honorable and capable leadership of West Point graduates. When there is division and mistrust among the home and foundation of America's military leadership, then deeply trouble times are ahead for America. The West Point of today is not the same academy as it once was. As America's political ideology and morality has changed, so too has West Point.

Considering that the Civil War has been a controversial subject for Americans in recent times as America's political views have changed, it is worth looking into this point of contention. The Civil War holds a personal closeness to me as my Jewish great-great-grandfather Joseph Beckhardt, born and raised in Bavaria, Germany, immigrated to New York City during the time of the American Civil War and thus served as a captain in the calvary in the Union Army. Indeed, there were also many other Jewish Americans who volunteered to serve in the Civil War—some even being awarded the Congressional Medal of Honor:

> Benjamin Levy
> David Urbansky
> Abraham Cohn
> Leopold Karpeles[2]

The Civil War was a sad and profound time in US history. West Pointers were truly at war with one another. Even Jefferson Davis, president of the Confederate States, was a West Point graduate. However, at the conclusion of the Civil War, both sides strived to find forgiveness and unity. Jefferson Davis, along with most other Confederate leaders received presidential pardons. The country wanted to move on and both sides looked at reconciling. However, now more than one hundred years after the Civil War, tensions are again at our doorstep due to the toxic liberal American ideology. The liberal Left's disdain for the Confederacy is so great that tearing down any monument is their solution. The liberal Left views Confederate statues as symbols of slavery, racism, and black oppression. If that were the case; then the Union statues should be viewed as symbols of freedom, integration, and black liberation.

I personally do not like seeing nor do I condone the Confederate statues being taken down. They are part of America's history. The Confederate officers were fighting for a different patriotic vision of America; and as we can all agree that slavery is immoral, I do not believe that slavery was the principle driving force behind the confederacy; however, they were still American patriots. If America wishes to tear down Confederate statues, then Union statues should go up in their place to honor the Union officers. This whole political affair is inappropriate and out of touch; all Civil War statues should be kept in place. Whatever your views are regarding the Civil War, it is part of American history. We can look back and disagree with some parts of American history, but we must take the parts with the whole and know that overall, America has been a beacon of freedom. Also, if you truly do not like America, then you are free to do what I did and leave the country.

If Americans cannot even stay committed in their own marriages,
Then how is it possible for Americans to stay committed to the country?

Americans are not even able to stay in committed relationships or marriages; with just only one other person; and this other person (Lover, Spouse, Soulmate, etc.) was initially such an ideal match for the other; however they still could not live together and continue to love each other. What would happen if divorce in America became illegal; that no matter how bad the marriage is; no matter how much domestic violence, no matter how much cheating and deceit, no matter how much either person despises or even hates the other one; these two people can never get a divorce and must live in the same home/house together for the rest of their lives. I predict the result would be a tremendous increase in murder rates between the spouses; as the union of marriage would get so dysfunctional and so hate filled; that either partner would eventually seek to kill the other; in an effort to free themselves from the prison of marriage; and thus allowing themselves to go on with their lives without the burden or hate from their now dead spouse. Although I do not advocate for divorce; I do however support that in America, divorce is legal; and as a result, there are even some occasions where a once hate filled marriage; turned into a friendly divorce. Where once the two people, having to live with each other, began to hate each other; however following the divorce; the two ex-spouses now get along very good. Each spouse moved on with their respective lives, living in separate homes, having separate bank accounts, and perhaps even living in separate parts of the United States. After each spouse was given the freedom from the other one; being no longer under the control of the other spouse; post divorce friendships are possible even between two once bitter ex-spouses.

Just as in a dysfunctional marriage, where divorce is the only safe and rational solution for the bitter and hate-filled spouses, America has turned into a dysfunctional country where a national divorce will be the only rational solution to prevent a violent civil war.

Likewise, sometimes a nation divided needs to look at all its options. The topic for a peaceful national divorce must be allowed for open discussion in the American media, politics, and society. As America continues to get more and more diverse, more and more Americans are desiring a political divorce. This peaceful divorce should begin with the moral and legal rights granted to all Americans.

Such a divorce is already happening organically as Americans are voluntarily moving to either conservative red states or liberal blue states. This is perfectly natural and should be supported by all Americans based on the principle of freedom and self-determination. All Americans should have the right to take back their private communities, even expanding and take the form of a state—as this is the natural progression.

As America becomes more and more polarized through forced diversity, sooner or later red and blue states respectively will begin to band together and seek a national divorce. Back in 2000, I began to see how the future of America would enter into more and more troubling times. The moral fabric of America was being pulled apart even during my time in the military. What is even more alarming is that Americans cannot even depend on the Military Officer Corps to provide them with strong and ethical leadership to successfully guide and protect America through this chaos that is about to eurupt. I was not at all impressed nor confident with the US military officer corps, as generally they were weak, godless men. They were low-testosterone corporate yes men just riding out their time to eventually obtain a cozy government pension. The American military officer corps through both their incompetence and immorality have lost the trust of the American people; they serve at the behest of the military-industrial complex, and do not stand with the American people. They have failed.

It is not the citizen's responsibility to inspire faith in the government; it is, however, the government's responsibility to inspire faith in the government.

This lack of trust in the government is one of the most essential reasons why I predict America will fall apart. As more and more American citizens lose faith in the government's ethics and competence, the systems and institutions in America will cease to function—especially when stress continues to increase due to financial hardships and/or violent threats.

It seems like America has two governments: the Democrats who represent and protect the liberal Left, and the Republicans who represent and protect the conservative Right. However, in most instances, the Democrats and Republicans are actually working in unison to represent and protect the American corporations. The politicians ultimately work for the globalist corporations. Therefore, once again there is a chance to unite Americans on both sides of the political spectrum. Instead of the media fanning the flames of division, it can bring Americans together by focusing on the two greatest enemies who are taking away the civil liberties of the citizens: big government and big corporations. They are the true enemies of the people regardless of whether you are a liberal lefty or a conservative righty. All Americans should rally around this cause to fight the real problems:

A continued and steady erosion of individual freedoms and American patriotism.

The American globalist government and American globalist corporations both have neglected the care and concern for American citizens' liberties and their sovereignty. We need leaders in America who can unite the country by demonstrating an unnerving reverence for personal freedoms and a patriotic love of America. By bringing the Left and the Right together, we then have a better way to resolve our problems, which may include a peaceful and respectful separation within America. The country has gotten so diverse, so multicultural that a national unification may already be impossible. We need to at least start the dialogue of a peaceful and respectful separation. American Citizens constantly complain about the partisan political infighting: how they are sick and tired of watching the Republicans and Democrats bicker and quarrel between each other and not work together to fix the real problems facing America and the American people. I am here to say; it is time for the American public to take responsibility for this problem, and for the Left and the Right to come together and admit:

We (Republicans and Democrats) don't get along with each other and We (Conservatives and Liberals) really want separation from each other.

America is like the married couple who has been in counseling for decades. The couple has reluctantly remained married; however, they both continue to express an intense disdain for one another and openly admit that they live in a dysfunctional and loveless marriage. They are both unhappy and miserable with each other. When the couple got married decades ago, they shared similar lives, cultures, ambitions, morals, and values. As time passed and both spouses grew older, however, they each began to drift in different directions. Now the two spouses do not share in the same cultures, ambitions, morals, and values. When they first met, they felt like they were both so much alike. Now they recognize that they are worlds apart. They don't even want to live with each other anymore, and they each constantly complain that the other one is always controlling them. They both need their own space, and they both want their own freedom once again. The marriage counselor has done his best over the decades to offer the couple a wide array of solutions and recommendations to solve their marital problems. Still there is no success or agreement in the marriage. The yelling and name calling has escalated into deadly threats. The marriage counselor now believes that the best solution, and safest solution, is for separation and divorce. By divorcing, each person will have the freedom to go their own way and make their own lives. Sometimes when this happened, although the divorcees may not claim to be friends, they usually admit that they do not hold any hatred for the other person and could be cordial with each other if they met at an event. Getting a divorce is nothing to be proud of, nor is it the goal of marriage. However, realistically sometimes a divorce may be the best option in a dysfunctional marriage where violence is highly probable.

As Americans continue to complain about the constant infighting between Democrats and Republicans, it is time to demand dialogue on the subject of a peaceful separation. This is already happening to some extent in America where citizens are fleeing from blue states to go live in red states. This voluntary migration has been called white flight, conservative flight, or Christian flight. It does not matter what the reason, every citizen should have the freedom to be able to relocate to any part of America and be able to voluntarily live with like-minded people. This is essential to the American dream of life, liberty, and pursuit of happiness.

As America continues to diversify, its citizens are no longer comfortable living in their current communities and want to relocate to like-minded communities. As this trend continues, states in America will continue to polarize along their respective political ideologies. Americans are going to expect more and better political governance at the state level, particularly from the governors of these states. Putting your state first will become more and more common as governors will be expected to put the citizens of their respective states before the country as a whole—to have loyalty to the citizens of their states above all others.

The deep polarization of the states will continue as the various state government organizations—governor, national guard, law enforcement, and representatives— reflect the values of the residents of that state.

That whenever any Form of Government becomes destructive of these ends, it is the Right of the People to alter or to abolish it, and to institute new Government
—Thomas Jefferson

As animosity toward the federal government continues to grow from both the liberal Left and conservative Right. Violence in the United States will surely increase with ever more fervor. This dwindling trust in the federal government will continue to wreak havoc on the systems and institutions that keep this country together. During these tense times, there will be many altercations between law enforcement and the citizens. There may even be altercations between the military and the Citizens.

My message to active-duty law enforcement and military is: Like you, I have served America in both my Army greens and police blues. I have never forgotten the legacy of our forefathers who fought and died in so many of America's wars and conflicts. They fought and died to preserve the precious freedoms granted to all American citizens. If the government takes away these precious freedoms, then what do we have left? Never forgot your oath and honor to that you took. Your ultimate service is not to the American Government, but to the American People.

One of America's most famous founding fathers, Patrick Henry, delivered his great speech on the rights of the colonies before the Virginia assembly. Henry is credited with having swung the balance in convincing the convention to pass a resolution delivering Virginian troops for the Revolutionary War. Among the delegates to the convention were future United States presidents Thomas Jefferson and George Washington. Patrick Henry's sentiment became the war cry for the patriots of the Revolutionary War:

Give me liberty or give me death.

American patriots should never forget America's roots and how our forefathers were willing to fight and die for freedom. Through your military and law enforcement service you carry on the torch of freedom that our great patriotic Founding Fathers have passed along to you. Never forget about all the patriots who died. They were your brothers, as well as mine. The statue of George Washington at West Point is a reminder of the courage of these brave men to fight valiantly, so we can live free. They were considered traitors by the British but heroes to Americans. They had the moral fortitude and internal strength to rebel against the tyrannical king of England. They put their love of country first, and many paid the ultimate sacrifice for it. Keep your patriotic spirit about you and never forget that the Sons of Liberty, our brave forefathers, have passed the torch of freedom to you. Therefore, if you are a patriotic law enforcement officer or military officer who is loyal to your oath to serve and protect your fellow American patriots, who will put your fellow patriots above all other peoples and institutions, then you are legally and morally justified to earn the respect from your fellow patriots. America needs your loyalty, and you need the loyalty of your fellow patriots. Together we will thrive and triumph through the patriotic blood of our American nation.

Patriotism is our oath;
Loyalty is our strength.

6

Fake Feminism: Weak Men Tolerate the Lie

Fake feminism is destroying the western way of life. It holds a negative view of men and has lobbied for big government to replace strong men. Fake feminists view the government as being responsible to protect women, eliminating the need for strong men in America, or the West for that matter. America will not survive unless we confront this falsehood.

Big corporations also try to replace strong men by convincing women to focus on their careers. They tell them that having a family is not important, so they don't need a strong man to be a husband and father. The relationship of men and women in a society and culture is paramount to that country's survival and prosperity. Liberal globalist ideology has programmed Western women into believing that they are being oppressed by patriarchy. This ideology convinces women that having a career will bring them the most happiness and that motherhood is a burden. All the while women slave away working for their corporate masters in a depressed state, falsely declaring they are happy as they see themselves getting older and the corporations getting richer from their sacrifices.

No promotions or accolades can compare to the joy and happiness of becoming a mother, spending time with your children, and helping your children grow and prosper. There is no greater love than a mother's love for her children. Thus, pressuring a woman to restrict her motherly instincts to fulfill this biologically preprogrammed dream will only lead down a dark and lonely path. As women's depression and prescription medicine use both continue to rise, American women continue to repeat the corporate mantra of Down with the Patriarchy; yet they secretly hope for a strong male superhero to come to rescue them from their depressing corporate robotic world and with whom they can build a family. They secretly long for a man to provide for both her and their children, a man to protect the family from the globalist evil that Western woman are slowly realizing is the real threat to America. They are awakening to the fact that danger and suffering are on America's horizon, and during dark times having a superman by your side is the best measure for a woman and her children's safety and security. If we are to diagnose the evil of liberal America and how it will contribute to the collapse of America, then we must talk about fake feminism.

Before we delve specifically into feminism, let us first look into America's noble principle of equal opportunity. Despite the concept of traditional gender roles, Americans should have an equal opportunity to apply and be hired to work in any job where you are able to meet the standards regardless of your gender, race, religion, age, or sexual orientation. The job standards should be the same for all regardless of your background. With that said, let me highlight some points:

1) American Citizens should have preferential treatment over foreign nationals. American Citizens should be favored for jobs that are:

a) Located on American soil regardless of whether the company is American or foreign owned.

b) American owned regardless of where they are located.

2) American employers should provide *equal* job opportunity and *equal* job standards. This is where discriminatory laws such as affirmative action should be abolished due to both racist and sexist favoritism. Favoritism should never be allowed in the public sector except for two points:

a) **Sacrifice**: Did the job applicant sacrifice him/herself in the name of patriot service: military service, volunteer service, religious service, a heroic act. If a person sacrificed themselves for the betterment of the American society, the applicant should be rewarded with preferential employment assistance.

b) **Disability**: Society; should exercise compassion and mercy. Being not of sound body or mind puts job candidates at a distinct disadvantage. Disability should be confined to the realm of either:

i) Hereditary disability due to a defect in the DNA. This is a disability completely out of the candidate's control.

ii) Innocent trauma that has permanently impaired the mental/physical constitution of the job applicant. Whether a person has suffered as a result of an accident or a violent attack, we have a responsibility to help this person deal with their trauma and offer preferential employment assistance to him or her.

iii) Self-inflicted injuries as a result of willful neglect or lack of responsibility from the person, such as drug addition, obesity, depression. Although society should offer programs to help all citizens deal with and overcome their physical/mental problems, it is primarily up to the individual to take care of themselves. Society may offer help in dealing with the problem, but no preferential treatment should be given to these people. They must take responsibility for their own actions and learn to fix the problems themselves.

Two Feminisms

There are two kinds of Feminism:

Fake feminism is found in 99% of the Western world. I say Western world as feminism primarily does not even exist outside the Western world. Therefore, in the West (America, Western Europe, Australia, Canada.) almost all of the feminism that exists is considered fake feminism. Fake feminism is the practice of demanding men and women be treated exactly the same—when it is in the best interest of women. On the other hand, fake feminism is also the practice of demanding men and women *not* be treated exactly the same—when it is in the best interest of women.

Fake Feminism combines *both* equal and unequal treatment in their ideology. Therefore, fake feminism is simply changing the standards of gender inequality to any outcome where the ultimate goal is that women are favored over men. Fake feminism is the prevalent feminist doctrine found in the West. I do not support this doctrine because it is fake. For one to enter the house of God, one must be real, and reality is truth. Fake feminism is a lie. Strong men will not tolerate this lie whereas low-testosterone beta males will tolerate this hypocrisy in their hopes of being sexually rewarded by these fake feminist women for championing their fake cause. Real feminism, though, is different. As you will see, almost all American/Western women do not support real feminism.

Real feminism is where men and women are treated 100% of the time in 100% of scenarios 100% equally.

Although I am against fake feminism, I fully support real feminism. Should America adopt real feminism it would actually be the women, as opposed to the men; who would be the leading voice to abolish feminism and adopt traditional conservative gender ideology. So let us examine some examples of how a society will look where real feminism (real equality) is fully administered.

Sports: Real feminism promotes only one sport's team. For example, there will be no more women's and men's soccer teams—just human soccer teams because in the end we are all human, according to liberal ideology. (This thinking will solve all the problems with transexuals as they too are humans.) The result of this will be that 99% of professional female athletes will be unemployed; the controversy of Transexual athletes will disappear; and finally most men will not even be effected. For example, in my case I am a boxer. Should a woman or a transexual boxer want to step in the ring with me, I don't have a problem with it. The odds will be heavily stacked in my favor. So real feminism wants true equality.

Toilets: Real feminism want to eliminate separate ladies' and men's rooms. Whether it is the locker room, changing room, shower, or toilet, they want to remove all gender discrimination and have only bathrooms for humans. Again, this solves the problem for transexuals. Who do you think will object to this policy more: men or women? I predict women will have a larger problem with this real feminist policy.

Prisons: Real feminism wants just one prison. No more women's and men's prisons, only human prisons. They want all male and female prisoners to be housed in the same detention centers—no separation or segregation based on gender. How do you think female prisoners will feel if they are housed with male offenders? Terrified is my guess. How do you think male prisoners will feel if they are housed with female offenders? Excited is my guess.

Military: Men will no longer be the only ones required to register for the draft or be drafted. Instead, all human beings will be required to register for the draft and be drafted. Furthermore, all military standards—physical fitness, dress codes, combat arms quotas, barracks arrangements, height and weight requirements, medical status, and more will be equally enforced upon all soldiers regardless of gender. Many of these same issues will also apply to emergency responders. And once again, this will solve all the issues relating to transexuals serving in the military. No more male and female soldiers—simply human soldiers.

College dorms: Co-education will be taken to new heights with real feminism. Colleges will not only all be mixed genders so will dormitories. Gender discrimination will not be allowed. Roommates will be seen as human rather than male, female, or transexual. College students will live, eat, shower, and sleep in a gender-neutral environment. College rape cases will increase of course.

Fashion industry: The new fashion industry will no longer have women or men's clothing; it will just be human clothing. No longer will modeling agencies be allowed to discriminate and hire more female models and pay women higher salaries. All models will be human; gender discrimination will not be allowed, and clothing will be gender neutral.

This list can go on and on. Understand that this feminist ideology is doomed for failure because it is detached from common sense. Men and women simply are different; they always have been and always will be. Leadership is generally both a male dominated domain and also a natural male attribute. In particular, politics, business, and military are specifically male-dominated fields because men have a more natural desire and inclination to compete, explore, and dominate; this is the byproduct of testosterone. Most women on the other hand prefer to let men do the leading—as well as the fighting and working—while they are provided for and protected, and most important , cherished, by men—and also given the luxury and happiness of motherhood.

For those women who do wish to pursue leadership careers, then by all means equal opportunities should be available but without preferential treatment. There will be anomalies, of course, and these women who succeed in leadership should be congratulated, however, most women prefer the men to do the leading.

One of the reasons for the decline in America's birthrate is the constant liberal push to have women in leadership positions, despite their general lack of competency and desire when compared with their male counterparts. This liberal dogma goes against the laws of nature as men and women, by their very own nature, are different and have their own unique strengths and weaknesses, as well as natural inclinations. Women are being pushed into the workforce with false promises of having a rewarding and fulfilling life as a professionally empowered career woman. Later on down the road, these now older single women end up depressed as they regret about their missed opportunity of becoming a mother and having a family.

My Body My Choice

There is one hot topic that must be addressed when discussing American women: abortion. This lightning rod of a subject needs to be clearly explained from the viewpoint of a freedom-loving patriot. I am pro-choice. I do not take this stance joyfully, but I believe in freedom. When Americans cannot be free to make choices concerning their own body, this should be a redline. If citizens do not have sovereign ownership over their very own body, then what is the point of freedom anyway?

The American feminist movement, however, has completely failed the American people with respect to the mandatory covid vaccinations. During the government's push to make covid vaccines mandatory would have been an excellent time for the liberal feminist Left and the freedom-loving patriotic Right to have formed a solid coalition. Both factions could have stood together with the slogan: My body, my choice. Whether the topic is abortion or vaccinations, both groups could support each other in their strong stance against government interference in sovereign body choices. Yet once again the fake feminist movement proved deranged, self-centered, and lacking any principles.

The primary reason why I support abortion is the notion of personal freedom and objection to government interference with a person's body. With that said though, I still have my objections with the current state of the abortion industry. The first being that the woman has the unilateral decision over the man; this imbalance of power needs to change. Specifically, women enjoy unequal legal status when it comes to child support and abortion. A pregnant woman can unilaterally decide whether to abort the fetus or not; and the man has no say. Yet, should the pregnant woman want to give birth to the child, the man is now legally obligated to pay child support—even though he may have wanted the woman to get an abortion. Should the pregnant woman want to have an abortion, the man has no say in the matter.

This unilateral power on the part of woman is not acceptable. As mentioned previously, I still support a woman's right to choose to have an abortion; however, just as a man cannot force a woman to have the child or abort the child, a woman should not have the legal power to force the man to pay for child support. If the woman desires financial child support, then she should either marry the man or have the man voluntarily sign a legal contract committing to financially supporting the child.

With regard to abortion, I support it with the following caveats:

The Sanctity of Life: I do not believe in the absolute sanctity of life. I believe in a soldier's duty to kill for country, a citizen's duty to kill to protect his family, a law enforcement officer's duty to use deadly force to neutralize a threat, the death penalty for a criminal, the request of a terminally ill patient to end their suffering. Death is a part of humanity and the path into and out of this earthly realm. What is more important is not death itself but the morality behind it, and can we, as a society, morally justify some types of killings over others?

Freedom: One of the evils of globalist communist ideology is the attack on our individual freedoms. Any attack on our freedoms must be viewed with paramount apprehension. We as human beings must always maintain sovereignty over our own bodies, whether that be from forced vaccinations or denying a woman her choice to abortion.

Morally Justified: The below cases of abortions are morally justified in my view, and the law should remain unchanged as to protect the woman's right of choice. These are cases of woman having an abortion due to:

- Rape or incest
- Mental or physical impairment of the fetus
- Danger to the health of the mother

Morally Unjustified: I do not support late-term abortions; these types of abortions should be illegal. Generally speaking, a woman should realize that she is pregnant within the first trimester. A woman needs to decide whether or not to have an abortion at that time. After the first trimester the woman should lose her legal right to have an abortion—unless later down the pregnancy either her health is in danger or a physical or mental impairment in the fetus is discovered. Otherwise, women must take responsibility and once her decision is made in the first trimester to have the child, then the woman should honor her promise to her unborn baby and follow through with the pregnancy.

Morally Ashamed: Abortion should never be morally justified as just a normal, practical, or conventional form of birth control. A woman who wants to have an abortion during her first trimester simply because she and her partner failed to practice safe sex is morally reprehensible and not what we want our society to accept or become. Even though I still legally support a woman's right to an abortion in this scenario, she should feel ashamed of her decision. In these scenarios taxpayer money should not be used to fund the procedure. The cost should be paid by the woman. Even if the woman's financial situation is so bad that she cannot afford the abortion, then at the very least, a reduced cost should be imposed. The woman should have to feel some type of financial hardship for undergoing an abortion. The American taxpayer should not be paying for these immoral procedures.

Prior to and following any abortion the woman should have to undergo mandatory counseling by the medical professional at the abortion clinic. This counseling should cover the seriousness of the abortion procedure, and it should be clearly and directly communicated to the woman that she will be condoning the killing of her unborn baby. Furthermore, immediately following the procedure the woman should be shown the actual dead fetus. Women, just like men, should learn to take responsibility for their actions and come face to face with the consequences.

The mandatory counseling should include specific recommendations for proper birth control methods, which should include abstinence, waiting until marriage, or, at the very least, raising their standards so that they only choose to have sex with a man with whom they would be willing to have a child out of wedlock. Women should never view abortion as a normal form of birth control.

God cannot be Everywhere at Once, that is why he Created Mothers —Jewish Proverb

---

It is amazing how coldhearted and indifferent feminists are to their own unborn child—how they can so easily kill their own child. However, if the topic is immigration or refugees, these same coldhearted feminist women immediately become devout loving caregivers. American feminists demand that Americans welcome and care for immigrants with open arms, regardless of whether or not they are women, children, or men. Despite the fact that these immigrants have no kinship with these American feminists—compared to their unborn babies—they have unconditional love to accept these immigrants into America and unconditionally care for them with the aid of taxpayer money. When it comes to abortion, these feminists are coldhearted. When it comes to immigrants, these feminists are warmhearted. In psychological parlance, this is called "self-hate" and is seen throughout America, not just with feminists.

Many of these feminists find themselves with no man, no marriage, no family, and no purpose in life, resulting in self-loathing. A career in corporate America will never fully fulfill a woman's desire for happiness like a family can, and this lack of family is behind American women's depression. Despite what the liberal media will try to convince modern American women, the truth is that not having a family will lead to a lonely life, especially when women pass the age of forty. Many of these lonely, hate-filled feminists will be suicidal due to their lack of family bonds.

In China, women have great pressure to get married and have children by the age of twenty-five. Upon nearing the age of thirty, Chinese women are anointed with the unflattering title of "leftover woman" （剩女）,[1] meaning; these women are undesired by men. They were not able to find a husband and get married, therefore, they are now the leftover women in society who will have an incredibly difficult hurdle in finding a husband. The dating culture in China can be construed as ruthless and intolerant; however, that is exactly what nature is. Nature is cruel and unforgiving, and within the context of romance and courtship, the laws of nature and attraction are in full force. What is actually cruel and unforgiving is lying to men and women about these laws of nature using some of the following fallacies:

- Women's promiscuity does not affect their attractiveness.
- Women's beauty and sexual attractiveness in their thirties and forties does not decline.
- Women's natural fertility to bear children in their thirties and forties is still fine.

Feminism has liberated women from the control of men. However, feminism should not liberate women from taking responsibility for their actions.

American women should never have been given the political right to vote unless they want to take on the equal and full responsibility of registering for the selective service like men. If American women are not willing to be drafted and go to war alongside their American male counterparts, then they do not deserve the right to vote. More specifically, women should be drafted into the same hazardous types of military occupations like frontline infantry, just like their male counterparts. Equal standards, equal responsibilities, and equal privileges.

All throughout the history of America women have been exempted from going to war and risking their lives in the defense of all the freedoms. American men have fought and died defending these rights. Women on the other hand have not only been exempt from mandatory military service, but more important, they have also been silent about this shirking of responsibility. During the Vietnam War, for example, American men were given the choice of going to war or going to jail. For an eighteen-year-old American man who was just months from being a mere teenage boy, to face either having to go overseas to kill or be killed or being sent to prison is an immense leadership challenge presented to such a young man. American women, on the other hand, were completely exempt from this national patriotic duty; however, women continued to demand equal rights, including their right to vote. If American women want the right to vote, then they must earn that right just like American men have to. Any American man who understands basic leadership principles and who also has at least a normal amount of testosterone in his blood would never permit American women to play their hoax of fake feminism. Real men would give women only one of two choices:

1) Equal rights and equal opportunities with equal standards and equal responsibilities.
2) Traditional roles where men and women are treated differently according to their gender.

In today's liberal American society, you have neither one of the above two options being exercised. On the contrary, fake feminism is the religion of choice in America and is corrupting society as a whole. It is similar to a spoiled child whose weak father enables the rotten behavior due to his aversion of disciplining the child.

American men have become so weak and effeminate that they lack the courage or strength to stand up to this unethical ideology of fake feminism. American fake feminists should hope and pray that the American system does not collapse, because despite popular opinion, the Western world is not a patriarchy; it is a matriarchy. No country in the world treats women better than Western countries like America. American women live a privileged life. Women, minorities, and immigrants are treated the best in Western countries, and specifically America. If it weren't for America's patriotic forefathers, who I am sure were full of toxic masculinity, America would never have been able to afford the privilege life offered to American women.

When men do not want to become soldiers and women do not want to become mothers, society will collapse.

7

Military-Industrial Complex: More Wars, More Profits

No longer are the days where the American military officer corps serves on behalf of the American citizens. Today's American military officers work on behalf of corporate America. President Eisenhower coined the phrase the "military-industrial-congressional complex." Using the word *congressional* was too inflaming, however. Therefore, Eisenhower was pressured to cut that word out, resulting in the now revised phrase "military industrial complex." American defense contractors need wars to keep their profit margins moving forward. War is about profits. That is why politicians, generals, and CEOs work in unison for their combined effort to convince the American public why yet another immoral war is justified in the so-called defense of the nation. More lies for more profits. Young American boys are persuaded to enlist in the military while the bulk of politicians, even though they advocate for war, neither themselves nor their children ever have any desire or intention of serving in the military. That is left for those Americans who are either underprivileged or overly patriotic; they are lied to by our government with phrases such as "serve your country," when in reality it is more like "serve the corporations." These enlisted servicemen pay the ultimate sacrifice and give their lives not in the name of nationalism and country, but in the name of American globalist corporations who relish in the fact that overseas markets can be opened up through the use of military campaigns. There is no end in sight regarding America's thirst for military conflict, The military industrial complex is a machine to which the American taxpayer is forced to feed, and into which young American boys are deceived into dying.

To the brave and loyal enlisted service members of the US Armed Forces, the American government owes you an apology. The military officers have failed you.

The generals and admirals have put their personal careers over the mission and the soldiers. The officer corps was entrusted with the sons and daughters of American patriots. The generals and admirals should never be trusted again.

Just short of twenty years and more than $2 trillion dollars the Afghanistan conflict was America's longest war, and it was a complete and utter failure. Any US general who labels that war a success or even a remote success is detached from reality. No one should blame the enlisted soldiers who fought in that war; they are honorable men and women who volunteered their service to the nation and dutifully obeyed the orders of their unethical commanding military officers.

Moreover, there were probably many battles to which these soldiers indeed achieved victory. However, with respect to the grand war, America simply lost and 100% of the blame should be placed on the flag officers; these generals are incompetent and unethical in their failure to accurately and candidly communicate to both the troops and to the American public the status and mission of the failing war campaign. All one has to do is remember the tragic story of the American patriot and US Army Ranger Pat Tillman and the lies and deceit that were promulgated by the unethical and cowardice generals in the aftermath of his death. Do not be fooled by the propaganda, the US military officer corps is filled with small-penis, low-testosterone, weak yes men, who lack the courage and candor to speak the simple truth when their careers are on the line. What is even more embarrassing about these generals is that they could not even accurately state what exactly was the mission in Afghanistan. If you asked a hundred different military officers, there would probably be a hundred different answers. And the American public was kept in the dark about what was the mission behind this war, which ended up costing the taxpayers trillions of dollars. When I was a graduate student at the Harvard Kennedy School, I met with numerous US national security scholars, and almost every time I would argue with these high-ranking, self-inflated egotistical government bureaucrats, I came away with the same impression: "These people are clueless." Whether they were with the military, intelligence community, state department, they almost all seemed confident that the war in Afghanistan was not only justified but that America would win. I always strongly stated that America would lose.

The War on Terror: Terrorists
The War on Crime: Criminals

This so-called war on terror was a hyperbole scam to get more funding for the military, government, and corporations. In history, as in life, there will always be terrorists, just like there will always be criminals. Both terrorism and crime can increase and decrease through the years; however, because of human nature we will never rid ourselves of terrorism or crime; that is the first thing to understand. The second point is to never underestimate crime prevention or terrorism prevention.

What is the US government doing overseas with regard to the American foreign policy? Creating hatred toward the United States.

The first thing to be aware of is that police officers deal with criminals; however, special operators deal with terrorists. Therefore, only a select type of professionals can successfully engage with and defeat terrorists. All conventional military forces that were deployed to Afghanistan should have stayed back in America to save the taxpayers money, to save their own lives, and to get them back to training for a major future conventional war like World War III. The conventional military is like a huge sledgehammer used to smash, kill, and destroy. Special operations, however, are finer and nimbler and can be called upon to conduct unconventional warfare that is suited to counterterrorism. Therefore, the two counterterrorism groups that are needed to combat terrorism are:

1. Special operators: Army Special Forces and Rangers and Navy Seals and Delta.
2. Intelligence community: FBI, CIA, NSA, DIA, and the like.

This counterterrorism taskforce is specifically designed in addressing terrorism. Just like the world will always need police officers to combat crime, the world will also always need special operators to combat terrorism. The best method for combating terrorism is similar to the best method for combating crime: through prevention. American citizens must evaluate what their country is doing overseas with regards to its foreign policy. It is turning foreign actors into foreign terrorists. Perhaps the most important strategy is for the American government to change its behavior overseas. Perhaps a change in America's foreign policy is the best way to reduce terrorism.

Looking back on the war in Afghanistan, during those twenty years, it is shocking how the American generals were not only promoted but called themselves leadership experts and were given consulting jobs in media, business, academia. These generals are delusional and unethical losers. They did not win America's wars. They are embarrassments to the military academies, which failed to properly train them on what true leadership entails.

During my time in the military, I had seen over and over again these so-called warrior leaders showcase a "courage under fire" leadership style, however, when it came to their own careers Jell-O is the best way to describe the consistency of their spines. Of course, there will always be exceptions to my critique.

One of my former military commanders who I prefer to maintain his privacy is Dave. He was an outstanding military leader and great role model. For so many years I have purposely avoided communicating with him as I did not want to get him or his family implicated into this unethical affair with the FBI. Dave treated me like a son and invited me into his family; I am truly honored to have served under his command. Dave was a big man with a big heart who was also a remarkable athlete at West Point. He set NCAA records and was later inducted into the West Point athletic hall of fame. During his time in the Army, Dave was not afraid to push his weight around and push back on higher command; however, this is what also cost him his promotion, and thus he was never selected for general.

Strong men many times get passed over for promotion, and it is the corporate yes men who many times make general. Today's generals have turned into corporate yes men. Their warrior ethos has been replaced with the docile, political nature that can be controlled by the defense contracting corporations and puppet politicians. These generals have lost the respect of their soldiers as they enjoy a nicely furbished retirement on the taxpayers' dime—all the while they continue to think they have some type of relevance in advising others on what it takes to become a great leader. These military generals and admirals have had their integrity compromised as they have failed to summon the courage to speak the truth as to what the U.S. military's intentions really are:

Get America into never-ending wars to reap never-ending profits and keep American taxpayers in never-ending debt.

In America, we have been brainwashed by much liberal propaganda. For example, liberals tell us diversity is our strength. They have also brainwashed us into thinking that democracy is the best form of government and therefore that America has the right to wage war with any non-democratic country in the world in order to transform them into a democracy. Don't get me wrong. I'm not knocking democracy. What I am stating is America has an imperialistic belief that every country on earth should be a democracy—even by strong military means. This American self-righteousness persuades the global community to view America as an imperialistic empire that forces other nations to bend to its will as opposed to allowing sovereign nations the right of self-determination. What is even more pathetic; is the fact that America's military campaigns to impose democracy on foreign nations have been an utter failure. Not only does America act as the world's bully, but it cannot even beat up its weaker opponents. It is time for the American government to worry more about the welfare of its own citizens as opposed to constantly meddling in the affairs of foreign nations. To illustrate just how powerful the military industrial complex is, and also just how easy the American public is to control, just look at these simple facts:

- America just finished the longest, most expensive, and most disastrous war in its entire history. As America pulled out of Afghanistan in one of the most embarrassing and disheartening ways imaginable, the American military industrial complex did not even miss a beat. America as a country did not even take time to reflect on how wrong we got the war in Afghanistan. No American general has yet to publicly apologize or admit to any wrong.
- American politicians have immediately declared how the Russia-Ukraine conflict is of vital interest to America and that

America will financially and militarily support Ukraine. Then these same loser generals appeared on the media, giving their so-called expert leadership advice on how America needs to get engaged in the conflict despite Putin's warning of nuclear war. These same war hawk politicians and incompetent generals who are both ultimately working for the American defense corporations are pushing America for yet another war despite the recent debacle in Afghanistan.

- Finally, America is yet again sounding the alarm on why the American taxpayer and US military must enter the potential war between China and Taiwan as well to defend Taiwan for the sake of America's freedom. Do you not see how the American military industrial complex is an unstoppable train wreck that will never cease in collecting its war profits through whatever manufactured American threat it needs. This train will never stop until it literally crashes and takes the entire country down with it.

To all the veterans who have returned home from Afghanistan wounded, and more important, to all the Gold Star families whose loved ones returned home in a casket, I ask all of you this question:

What freedoms were you and your loved ones fighting to defend when even the basic freedom of speech in America is no longer protected?

In America, our own civil liberties are under attack; our own individual freedoms are being taken away by the government and corporations. Therefore, what "American freedoms" were our soldiers fighting for in Afghanistan, Iraq, Syria? In fact, the American soldiers were not fighting on behalf of the American citizens; they were pawns fighting for the American defense corporations greedy pursuit of higher profits. Furthermore, they were being led by the unethical and incompetent generals and politicians who are beholden to these globalist defense corporations. The reason why the American generals and politicians failed the soldiers, and also the America people, is because they no longer possess and exhibit the three basic foundational elements which are essential to leadership:

1. **Courage:** Bravery is not an optional quality for leaders. Leaders must have the courage to stand up to adversity; if not, they will shirk their ethical duty to the mission and to the people in favor of personal safety and security. Courage doing what needs to be done in the face of physical injury or death, in the face of job loss or demotion, in the face of reputational damage and negative criticism, or in face of a loss of those things or people you deeply care about. There is a continuous decline in courage from western men and this should sound alarm bells as weak, cowardly men are more prone to commit unethical acts and choose what's easy over what's right.

2. **Intelligence:** As a leader, you are not expected to be the subject matter expert or technical professional for many of the operations that you oversee. A leader will rely on his managers and professionals for the technical details; he will trust in their expertise to negotiate the obstacles in their industry lanes. What a leader is expected to have, however, is an acute understanding of the grand strategy, an uncanny ability in grasping the overall operation, which will lead to mission success. The leader is expected to have a PhD in common sense learned through real-world experience. A

leader's emotional intelligence should reign supreme in his
ability to gauge people's mindsets and anticipate their
behavior. This includes all of his key stakeholders, from his
allies to his adversaries, from his inner circle confidants to his
outer circle customers. A leader does not have to be smart
enough to understand all the parts of the machine; however,
he must be smart enough to understand the holistic system to
which the machine operates in.

3. **Loyalty:** A person who is both courageous and intelligent
    will surely be a success in life; however, these people many
    times are in fact sociopaths, because they may have no ethical
    considerations for others, nor do they have a moral compass
    that points anywhere other than in the direction of their own
    personal ego. Regarding the ethics of a leader, it boils down
    to loyalty. The leader must be loyal to his people and to the
    overall team/ organization/ company/ country. If the people
    sense that the leader is disloyal, then they will not follow him.
    This is exactly the problem in America regarding the ideology
    of globalism; the politicians and CEOs are increasingly
    putting the interests of American citizens and the country
    behind that of foreign nationals and foreign nations. This lack
    of loyalty is a recipe for disaster. If it continues, an American
    collapse or civil war is inevitable. Leaders must be loyal.

**Leadership at its peak involves the
negotiation with death at the table.
Therefore, leaders must be ready for death's
unwillingness to walk away from the table.**

During my initial entry into the military, I learned an important
leadership lesson as well as a solemn reminder of life's ultimate rally

point. Although horrific in nature, it was beneficial that I learned this leadership lesson early in my life. During my first couple of months into my first semester at MMI, it was a weekday evening around eight o'clock. It was mandatory study period, and all cadets were required to be in their rooms, studying at their desks. All doors to the rooms must be completely open at ninety-degree angles, and loud talking was not permitted. MMI cadets lived in military barracks with a single long hallway per floor with rooms on either side, so you could see into the room directly across the hallway. A senior cadet would be on duty as the hall monitor. His job was to enforce the rules and discipline of the study period. He would either sit at a desk in the middle of the hallway or patrol the area for any infractions. If a cadet needed to go to the latrine, for example, he would need to ask permission from the hall monitor in order to leave his room.

Normally, there were two cadets assigned to a room; however, I was alone in my room as my roommate had quit MMI a month prior; the room across the hall from mine also had only one cadet in it. We will refer to him as Cadet X. Cadet X's roommate decided to study at the library that night, which was authorized. So therefore, Cadet X and I were both alone in our respective rooms. As I sat at my desk studying, I could clearly see Cadet X studying at his desk as both of our doors were required to be fully open. The total distance between us was approximately eight meters.

Sometimes out of boredom, or as a means to reduce the stress of cadet life, the cadets on opposite sides of the hallway would attempt to communicate with each other using various forms sign language (sometimes vulgar and funny in nature) or even risk throwing paper notes across the hallway to the cadets on the other side. It was like being locked up in prison. For example, there is a type of "Lord of the

Flies" culture where cadets try to physically dominate each other; the upperclassmen act as the wardens keeping the lower class cadets in line through their own use of hazing and intimidation.

I remember all the stressful thoughts going through my head as I was trying to plan, organize, and schedule my cadet life and academic workload to meet all the standards required for MMI, Army ROTC, and West Point preparatory. Sometimes it truly felt overwhelming and so confusing as I lacked the wisdom to understand and navigate through all the overwhelming obstacles that cadets face on a daily basis. A leadership lesson on how to see through the fog was vital in my future development as most cadets undergo a greater amount of stress than normal college students. The stress is necessary toward the cadet's leadership development; however, as anyone can foresee, too much stress can eventually push anyone to his or her breaking point.

During that night, as usual, I would sometimes turn my head to look over at Cadet X to see what he was doing—just a mild form of entertainment during my study breaks. I saw Cadet X with a handgun in his hand. At first, the sight of a handgun did not shock me, since being in the military for a couple of months and all. I wasn't sure, though if a handgun was authorized or not in the barracks room, but by no means was I alarmed. I occasionally turned back and forth from my studies to look across the hallway and see what Cadet X was up to or attempt to communicate with him as to relieve my stress and boredom. When I looked at him, I saw him pointing and dry firing his handgun. Occasionally he would look at me with a blank stare as if nothing was wrong. I motioned to him with my hands as if asking him, "what are you doing?" He paid no attention to me as he continued to calmly fidget with his gun, going through all the routine maintenance checks on it. I did not know Cadet X very well, and I would not say we were good friends, so I was not knowledgeable of his personality. I went back to my studies. After about fifteen minutes or so of looking at my books, I took yet another study break and turned in my chair again to look across the hallway at Cadet X. He was now sitting in his chair by his desk; however, he looked as if he was pointing his gun to his head. I was stunned.

He then turned and looked at me with his gun pointed at his head. I threw up my hands and silently mouthed the words "what are you doing!?". The whole scene was like an eerie dream or movie as I had no idea what was going to happen next. He then turned away from me with the gun still to his head, and I just sat there staring at him from across the hallway at him. I was fixated on him, still trying to analyze what was going on. Then suddenly, I heard a pop. I was already well accustomed to the sound of gunfire; however, this pop sounded more like a firecracker, so I was not sure what I had just witnessed. I immediately jump to my feet. Now 100% of my attention was on the scene across the hall. Cadet X's body immediately slumped over after the popping sound, and I could hear the upperclassman hall monitor shout throughout the hallway: "who the fuck lit the firecracker!?"

Seconds passed as I continued to stare at Cadet X and then I could see the faint sight of red liquid oozing from his head, which was slumped over on his desk. It quickly dawned on me "that is blood, and Cadet X just shot himself." I immediately ran to the edge of my door but was still disciplined and intimidated enough to not cross the threshold without the permission of the hall monitor. I now stared at the body of Cadet X. It became very clear that he had indeed shot himself. I poked my head out of my doorway and turned to the hall monitor who was marching down the hallway to find what he still thought was the firecracker culprit. I shouted to the hall monitor. "Sergeant, I think Cadet X shot himself."

"Did you light the fucking firecracker Baumblatt!?"

"No, Sergeant! I think Cadet X shot himself!" This time the hall monitor understood what I had said, and his demeanor suddenly changed. He rushed into Cadet X's room. I was still standing at the edge of my doorway, still too nervous to leave my room without permission. I could see the hall monitor quickly inspect the body of Cadet X, and in a matter of seconds he came running out of the room shouting, "Everyone, close your fucking doors! Get in your fucking rooms! All doors closed, now!"

He began yelling the names of senior upperclassmen to get down there immediately. My door was slammed shut by upperclassmen cadets now in the hallway; however, I put my ear on the inside of the door to listen to what was going on outside. Soon, I could hear the voices of the numerous upperclassmen in the hallway and especially right outside my door as they converged on Cadet X's room.

They continued yelling at us to shut our doors. "I don't care if you need to go to the latrine. Piss out your fucking window!" "Quite! Everyone shut the fuck up!"; then I would hear doors slamming. I could hear upperclassmen talking amongst themselves about getting an ambulance and administering first aid. As I was listening with my ear to the door, all of a sudden my door was violently pushed open, knocking me in my head. Three upper-class cadets barged into my room in absolute interrogation mode. I immediately snapped to attention and began to receive a battery of questions regarding what I saw. After about five minutes, I answered all their questions directly, and the upperclassmen were satisfied with my answers; then they left my room and forgot to close my door all the way. I could now see the paramedics putting Cadet X onto a gurney. In a matter of seconds Cadet X was taken to the ambulance and transported to the local hospital. The next day, the upper-class cadets informed us that Cadet X had died in the hospital due to a gunshot wound.

Death is a topic that leaders must be comfortable to talk about and must never forget that at any moment and on any given day death may decide to refuse to walk away; then you will find yourself in your final negotiation with life. Make sure you are always ready to negotiate with death. Your best tools will be honor and courage.

> **A soldier is willing to die to protect the freedoms that the flag symbolizes. A soldier is also willing to die to protect a citizen's right to burn the flag.**

Before I end this chapter on America's imperialism, I would like to address a post-World War II reality in which America became the global superpower and thus the world's police through the threat of military force. Despite America's self-imposed moral high ground, America is so far the only country in history to deploy nuclear weapons, dropping two atomic bombs on Japan. If America would have lost the war, America never would have been allowed to have nuclear weapons again, and the officers responsible for dropping the two atomic bombs on Japan would have been tried as war criminals and summarily executed. American children would grow up reading about the atrocities committed in Japan by the evil American aggressor; they would be filled with guilt and shame as American teachers would be required to educate the students on all the evil deeds committed by the American military during WWII. American students would also be educated about the Japanese internment camps into which the American government forced Japanese-American citizens to live as prisoners. The world would have shamed America for its atrocities and evil deeds, and America would have never been allowed again to take any leadership role in world affairs.

With victory, however, comes the spoils of war—the privilege of writing the history. This is why there is no guilt in America regarding the genocide of the Native Americans. European Americans won and the Native Americans lost; therefore, there shall be no guilt on the hands of today's Americans. This is the luxury and the allure of power: might makes right.

As a leader contemplates what is the morally right path, he must never forget that human beings are quite inflexible when it comes to survival. We as a people and as a nation will almost always choose the path that ensures our survival regardless of the morality and ethics. Where there is superiority of power, there is also superiority of morality. This is the ominous omen of America. Should it cease being the economic and military superpower of the world, then America will no longer have the power to impose its moral superiority on the world. Leadership is a dangerous endeavor to which only the victorious survive. In America's case, as long as it has the guns and the gold, it will reign supreme—not because of its moral superiority, but because of its economic and military superiority.

The victorious man will lay judgement upon the defeated man. However, in the end all men will ultimately be judged by God and God alone.

8

Defund the Police: From Community Hero to Government Bully

Police officers used to be considered heroes in America. Now they are bullies, and this label is now appropriately deserved in a general sense. Spokesmen for US law enforcement continue to give the same excuse over and over: the vast majority of officers are good people; however, there are just a few bad apples. My response is: Why can you not catch these few bad apples in your departments? Are you lazy, incompetent, or do you actually refuse to catch them? The focus should be on changing the management and policy within US law enforcement agencies as opposed to weeding out the bad cops. Law enforcement has lost the trust of the American people.

> **It is time for law enforcement to stop policing the American public and start policing their own rank and file first.**

Republicans want to go strong on crime, and this spurs them in fully supporting law enforcement by increasing both the numbers of police officers and expanding their police powers. This is absolutely

the wrong direction to go; it will backfire. What the country does not
need is more police officers, which citizens must pay for, and it
definitely does not need to increase their powers. Law enforcement has
forgotten that they are sworn to serve and protect the American
citizens. During my time in the FBI, one particular mentor was a
seasoned field agent and Vietnam veteran. He took pride in his military
service. He summed up his disdain for the tyrannical FBI management
in a few words:

The FBI is like the great white hunter shooting at wounded animals.

It is time for the American citizens to standup to law enforcement
and remind them that their job is to serve them. I propose a 50% cut
in law enforcement funding. All societies and countries need police
officers. As long as there is crime, society will always need police
officers; this fact will never change. Defunding the police by 50%,
however, will send a strong message to law enforcement management
that the citizens are not satisfied with their unethical behavior. By
downsizing police by 50%, this will give the leaders the opportunity to
finally get rid of all the "bad apples" they claim to unintentionally
harbor. The following two protocols should address the issue of crime
and safety due to the reduced number of police officers patrolling the
streets and on duty:

1. **Embrace the Second Amendment**: Every American
   citizen has the right to bear arms and the duty to defend
   himself, his family, and his community. The Second
   Amendment is the most important constitutional right

granted to American citizens, because without this right, all the other constitutional rights can and will be so easily taken away by the government. The Second Amendment is a citizen's best protection against both a violent criminal, but more important from a tyrannical government. An armed public won't have to depend as much on Law Enforcement to protect them from violent encounters.

2. **Allow Americans to take back their communities**. It is time for Americans to be allowed to fully retake ownership of their private communities and put an end to the federal government's control over the citizen's private lives. Private homes, businesses, schools, organizations. It is time for Americans to have the freedom of choice in their private lives. To have the freedom to choose who they want to associate with and who they want to allow into their private lives and homes. American's need the freedom to take back their private communities.

Forced segregation is unethical and illegal.
Forced integration is also unethical and illegal.

Regarding discrimination, consider when one chooses the person they want to marry. It would be ridiculous if the government intervened to curtail "discrimination." For example, as a heterosexual man, I would willfully discriminate against all men when looking for a spouse. What if a woman chooses to marry only a tall man and thus discriminates against all short men. Or a Christian chooses to marry only another Christian. Or what if someone wants to marry a person of a certain ethnic race. If the government got involved in legally restricting who someone can and cannot marry, we would all think that is tyrannical and an absurd encroachment by the government on American citizens' personal lives and freedoms.

Americans should be allowed to discriminate using whatever criteria they personally want to use with regard to their own private lives. The United States government should not have the legal power to control who American citizens can or cannot associate with regarding their private lives. This is a mark of freedom; forced integration is unethical and illegal within the confines of private institutions. By granting Americans the freedom to choose who they will associate with in their private affairs, the government rightfully returns to the citizens the freedom to shape and manage their private communities in a manner how they see fit. This right to association extends to private homes, private businesses, private schools, and private organizations.

Regarding a citizen's public life, however, any organization that receives federal subsidies—public schools, public organizations, public corporations, public housing—should not have these unrestricted legal freedoms. Public entities must abide by government regulations regarding forced integration. However, as stated above, private communities should be allowed to order their own "home"; and human beings naturally prefer homogenous environments. It is time for American citizens to take back ownership of their communities and to transform them into homogenous communities of like-minded citizens. These homogenous communities will experience a rapid decrease in crime. Coupled with armed citizens living in homogenous communities, the need for law enforcement will decline.

Private Entities: Unrestricted Discrimination of Individuals' Choices
Public Entitles: Restricted Discrimination of Individuals' Choices

Taking these above two theories into account, let us look at an example of Big Tech censorship of certain groups or individuals who have been de-platformed or censored on YouTube, Twitter, Facebook, and other social media platforms. When people like President Donald Trump and others US citizens are censored on these platforms, the liberal groups supporting Big Tech usually present this argument: "it is the right of the Big Tech companies to censor whoever they want since it is their business; these corporations should be allowed the freedom to pick and choose who they want to allow on their platforms or not."

If these technology companies were private companies, then yes, I would agree with this argument. As I have already stated, private American companies should have the legal authority to choose with whom they would like to associate whether that be with their employees, customers, or vendors. Private companies must be given the unilateral legal authority to discriminate however they see fit. The problem lies with the fact that these tech companies are not private. They are publicly traded corporations, and therefore the US government should step in to enforce the law. Public corporations like YouTube should not be legally allowed to censor its content creators based on some vague internal, unilateral, subjective criteria; this unjust practice is in violation of the First Amendment. Under current law, companies and corporations are legally able to discriminate according to some criteria; however, they are not legally able to discriminate according to other criteria. For example, some categories encompassing legal or illegal discrimination include:

Gender

Political Affiliation

Race

Nationality

Sexual Orientation

Hate Speech

Religion

Age

Conspiracy beliefs

Some people may not agree with being legally allowed to discriminate against everything on the list; some may want to add or delete certain categories, and by law, there are certain categories which are illegal to discriminate against (e.g., race, religion, and gender) in America. Why are some of the above identifiers protected by law and others are not? The answer is simply because we as Americans have agreed upon these identifiers (at least most of us) many decades ago and then the US Supreme Court has ruled to affirm these are protected categories; then laws were passed and even the Constitution got ratified.

Do not fool yourself. It is not judges, lawyers, or politicians who are the originators of the laws in America. It is ultimately the American people who decide what is moral and legal in America. And as the American public changes, so too do the American views on morality, which will then affect the legal system. Then the Constitution is only as viable or strong as the American people want it to be. Never forget that the power of a country always rests in the people, and more specifically the people who are willing to fight and die for the nation.

Going back to the original argument about company censorship, if the tech firms were private companies, then I would agree with their right to censor whomever they want for whatever reason they want. However, this is not the case in America as private business owners cannot censor their customers for any reason. For example, you cannot simply deny customer service just because you do not like the ethnicity of your customers; that would result in a lawsuit, and you will eventually be shut down unless you reverse your course of action. These are constraints put on American businesses. Consider these two scenarios:

Using affirmative action for hiring and censoring politically Right views on YouTube is legally justified discrimination.

Denying customer service to LBGT people and renting an apartment only to a certain ethnic group is NOT legally justified discrimination.

The result is Americans are feeling that the justice system is not treating people fairly. Some groups are legally allowed to be discriminated against, while other groups not allowed to be being discriminated against. The justice system is losing its sense of equal justice under the law for all people. The solution:

A public company *does not* have the right to refuse service to any customer for any reason.

A private company *does* have the right to refuse service to any customer for any reason.

American citizens should have the right to take back ownership of their *private* communities, which would include all private institutions. Private companies should not have any restrictions imposed from the American government regarding who they can and cannot serve. Therefore, a *private* technology company would be absolutely permitted to censor President Donald Trump or any other person for any reason they deem appropriate.

During my over ten years of living in China, I witnessed two very stark and correlating features: safety and homogeneity. Regarding violent crime, China was not even close to America. During my entire time in China, I never felt threatened by any criminal violent encounter, which is much more common in the United States. Even China's mega-cities, such as Beijing or Shanghai, are essentially free from violent crime. They are so safe in fact that a young woman could walk home alone on the streets of Beijing or Shanghai in late hours of the night and never have to worry. China was just that safe; it was absolutely remarkable. Most western expats have made similar observations about the low violent crime rate. The single biggest factor to China's low violent crime rate is China's remarkable level of homogeneity as compared to America. Chinese communities are filled with, well, Chinese; there is an absolute absence of diversity. These communities of like-minded Chinese citizens who almost all share the same cultural norms, which results in a low level of violent conflict.

We should not look at this lack of diversity negatively. I am not proposing that every single community in America must be exactly the same. America can offer the freedom to have as many different kinds of communities as possible; however, each community will most likely become homogeneous on its own based on the local citizens' personal desires. For example, the Chinatowns located in America in and of themselves are naturally homogenous as Chinese Americans prefer to live in Chinatown. Now, not every community will be a Chinatown, but every community in America will probably become more homogenous (filled with like-minded people) through the freedom of association. America as a whole can still be home to a diverse array of different kinds of homogenous communities. This is what we are seeing with the conservative red states and liberal blue states. People naturally want to live in communities of like-minded people. Think…

Monoculturalism on the community level.
Multiculturalism on the national level.

By banning forced integration, American citizens will have the freedom to build safe and caring homogenous communities of like-minded citizens. This will reduce the instances of so-called gun violence in the country. The first issue that the liberal left gets wrong with regarding gun violence in America is the word *gun*. One should first take the word *gun* out of the phrase and say just violence in America. Americans must come to terms with violence in their country and ask why.

Whether violence is being committed with or without a weapon is not the issue; the issue is violent crimes as a whole. Let's understand that first and then we can discuss the gun issue. If a society becomes more and more violent, then of course the offenders will use whatever weapons are available to them. The question is why is America so violent? Through my world experiences, I believe it is due to forced integration or forced diversity. That is the primary reason for the violence in America.

As forced diversity in America increases, so too does the rate of violent crime. We have already seen that China is a safe and homogenous country; however, China is also a country where firearms are banned. Perhaps some readers will point to the fact that the ban on guns is the reason why China is so safe. Allow me to use Switzerland as another example. I completed my MBA in Switzerland and while living in the country, I had the chance to experience yet again a country that is far safer than America. However, unlike China, Switzerland does allow gun ownership. In fact, Switzerland has the second-highest rate of gun ownership among developed countries outside the United States.

Here's what you need to know about the Swiss gun culture. From being the world's second biggest weapons exporter per capita to having the highest gun ownership rate of any European country, Switzerland has a relatively strong pedigree when it comes to weapons. The nation of 8.3 million people has approximately 2.3 million guns, giving it the third highest gun ownership rate in the world after the United States and Yemen. Approximately 48 percent of Swiss households have at least one gun. With gun ownership being so high in Switzerland, why don't you see the similar percentage of mass shootings and violent crime rate as you do in the USA? The simple fact is because Switzerland is generally a homogenous European society. It is not nearly as diverse as America. The answer again is monoculturalism versus multiculturalism.

One day, I hope Americans will have the courage to speak the truth; and the truth is that forced diversity is not a strength; it is a weakness, and a danger to society. It is also immoral and should be illegal. The safest place a human being can be is in his home, and home is defined by being around people just like you. Living in like-minded communities, along with the right to bear arms, will make America safer than living in a multicultural society with an ample number of police officers.

US law enforcement is not racist.
US law enforcement is tyrannical.

The primary problem with law enforcement is not racism. The problem is their tyrannical power and authority they wield over all Americans, regardless of race.

Take George Floyd for example. What Derek Chauvin did was atrocious to say the least. And although I am a very race conscious person in how I see the world, when I first saw the images of Officer Chauvin kneeling on the neck of Mr. Floyd, I initially did not even think about race at all. I simply pictured a tyrannical police officer abusing an American citizen. Instead of Mr. Floyd being pinned to the ground choking, I imagined one of my friends in that same position. I was absolutely furious. It is yet another prime example of why the Police need to be defunded. Regarding race, however, if Mr. Chauvin happened to be black or Mr. Floyd happened to be white, this case would have probably never have made national news—and definitely would not have had the political impact it has had to this day. White Policemen are abusing white men, and black policemen are abusing black men and so on. This is not about police discrimination. This is about police abuse. For those who disagree with me, I can assure you that my proposal to defund the police takes into account racism. As I have stated earlier, American citizens deserve the right and freedom to take back their neighborhoods and build safe and caring homogenous communities. These homogenous communities should be served by like-minded police officers. Since the defunding of the police will only be around 50%, there will still be policing in communities. So who are these police officers:

1. **Sheriff's Department**: Unlike most law enforcement officials, sheriffs are usually elected and are accountable directly to the citizens of their county. Therefore, the citizens of these homogenous communities will usually end up electing sheriffs who share their values. Homogenous communities will elect like-minded sheriffs, resulting in decreased friction between the citizens and law enforcement, thus increasing overall satisfaction from the citizens.

2. **Integrated Police Officers**: Standard police officers are responsible for policing these American communities and should also conform with these communities wishes. For example, communities should be able to hire their police officers based on the factors that make them homogeneous—whether these factors are based on race, religion, politics, sexuality. The police officers assigned to these communities should also reflect these factors for two reasons: First, the taxpayers deserve proper representation and service from the government. Second, the government officers will avoid all the discrimination conspiracy theories relating to law enforcement when you have white police officers policing white communities and black police officers policing black communities. The result will eliminate any suspected bias policing.

Securing the border is national security, and all illegals entering the US must be stopped immediately.

The elements of law enforcement that should not be defunded, and in fact should be expanded, are the US Coast Guard and US Customs and Border Protection (CBP). The American government must take responsibility in securing the border and thus preventing all and any illegal immigrants, as well as illegal contraband, from entering the United States. That the government is unwilling to secure the border, including all entry and exit points, such as international airports, from illegal foreigners is an outright crime against the American taxpayer and puts the security and welfare of all citizens at risk. Regarding secondary security inspections at the border, the CBP agents should be given as much authority as needed to properly screen foreign nationals. Regarding US citizens, however, the CBP should no longer be authorized to conduct secondary security screenings or any type of interrogations unless there is probable cause that a crime has occurred or is about to occur. Regarding my personal experience at O'Hare Airport, no citizen should ever have to undergo that type of treatment at hands of the US government without probable cause of a criminal act. I did not serve in the military so I could have my constitutional rights stripped from me as I enter or exit America. On the contrary, I expect all US citizens to be granted unimpeded access into and out of the United States—unless probable cause of a crime is present. In addition, in America US law enforcement should have increased legal powers when monitoring, policing, and investigating foreign nationals; however, decreased legal powers when dealing with US citizens.

An attack on a US citizen is an attack on America.
US law enforcement must ensure foreigners do not pose a threat to US citizens.

There is a very important rule in China for foreigners, one that a foreigner will never want to break: never, ever physically assault a Chinese citizen. The circumstances are almost irrelevant, even including self-defense. It does not matter. A foreigner must never physically assault a Chinese citizen. Should this happen, the aftermath of such an event will be swift and the punishment harsh—immediate imprisonment followed by immediate deportation of the foreigner from China. An example of this occurred while I was living in Chengdu, Sichuan （成都，四川）.[1] A Canadian expat was walking across the street when a Chinese driver illegally ran through the red traffic light. He hit the expat in the cross walk, knocking him to the ground and injuring his leg. The expat angrily got up and limped over to the Chinese driver, who was still seated in his car. In a rage, the expat began punching the Chinese driver who had rolled his window down. This incident was all caught on video and led to a police investigation. During the trial, the Canadian pleaded his case about how he suffered physical injuries due to being struck by the car when the Chinese plaintiff illegally ran the red light. The result was that the Canadian was jailed and then immediately deported from China, never allowed to return to China again.

In China, the government ensures that no foreigners living in China will ever be a physical threat to the Chinese citizens. This is absolutely not tolerated. The government always puts the safety and welfare of its citizens above foreigners. Compare this to both America and Western Europe where refugees, immigrants, and foreigners attack, rape, and terrorize the local citizens with little serious consequences. The reactions range from condemning the local citizens themselves as racists to handing down extremely light punishments to the foreign attackers. In contrast the Chinese government ensures its citizens are safeguarded from any violence committed by foreigners.

If you want more criminals, make more laws.
—Daoist Proverb

The liberal globalist American government and corporations want to replace strong men. There is such an obvious discrimination and bias against strong, European, heterosexual, Christian, white men. Throughout history men were expected to provide for and protect the women and children. Through big government and big corporations, the American public has been indoctrinated to believe that strong men are no longer needed nor wanted. They are taught that big government and big corporations can and will replace strong men. The globalists want to convince Americans that the best solution to keep them safe is with a robust police force and that American men are incapable of protecting their women, children, families, and communities. The truth is, however, that American patriots do not need the police to protect their communities.

American men are capable and willing to become the heroes of their communities, to put themselves in the path of danger to protect their people. What young American men desire is more freedom and less police. It is time to **Make American Men Strong Again**. Any American man who is "afraid" for his safety because the police are not there to protect him is not an American patriot. The only thing American patriots need to protect themselves and their people is freedom. It is time to give back freedom to American men and allow them the individual responsibility in protecting their women and children.

If a woman happens to be a real feminist, then she should be able to handle this responsibility as "equally" as a man can. If a woman happens to be a traditional conservative, then she will find a strong man to be her gallant knight to protect her in times of danger. To American women, the choice is yours:

> **Liberal America**: When the ship is sinking, it is only the children who are allowed first onto the lifeboats. Women, just like men, will have to wait your turn in line as you will be treated just like a man If you die, then you die like a man.
> **Conservative America**: When the ship is sinking, it is women and children who are allowed onto the lifeboats first. The men will have to wait behind. and if they die, then they will die because it is a man's duty to put the lives of women and children before his own.

**You can still be pro law enforcement,
just be against law enforcement's attack on
civil liberties.**

9

U.S. Intelligence Community: Spying, Lying, and Hiding

It is amazing that the US government provided false intelligence to the world regarding weapons of mass destruction in Iraq. What's more amazing is no one in the intelligence community was terminated due to this utter failure and American government leaders who were directly responsible for this illegal and immoral Iraq War—former Secretary of State Colin Powell, former President George W. Bush, and former Vice President Dick Cheney—are considered to be great American leaders and patriots.

To think of all the American tax money spent funding these corrupt American defense corporations so these globalist corporate executives and politicians can continue to live their rich and elite lifestyles. It's despicable how much money and lives the Americans have sacrificed for the imperialist globalists. They have ruined the reputation of America from an image of a free-peaceful democratic country to an imperialistic globalist empire hellbent on military conflicts to feed its insatiable appetite for profits.

It is amazing that the American people still have faith in the US intelligence community, or the government for that matter. As a former US counterintelligence officer, I certainly have no faith in our government due to its unethical and incompetent behavior and actions.

Proponents of the government like to point out the intel community is actually very competent, but because the classified nature of its successes, we can't know about them. Yet somehow only the failures are made public. This is just another lie told to the American public, so their tax money can continue to support the inept and unethical classified and covert operations of the US intelligence community without the American people having any oversight or knowledge on how much of their tax money is being wasted.

Most of the so-called China experts working in the US intelligence community are far from experts. Remember, this is the same intel community that consistently flip-flops on its intelligence threat analysis facing America. For example, after the 9/11 terrorist attack, the US intelligence community declared that radical Islamic terrorism was America's greatest threat. Then it changed to Russia, then to China, then to climate change, and now it is domestic terrorism from white supremacists. Incompetent and immoral is how I describe the US intelligence community. When I was in the FBI, I adamantly declared to management that China was a much bigger threat to America than radical Islamic terrorist; however, FBI management routinely dismissed me. The reason was due to immorality and ineptitude. At the time, America was in a kinetic war with Iraq and Afghanistan. As opposed to a non-kinetic spy war with China. Therefore, all one had to do is follow the money; there are bigger profits to be made by the American defense contractors in a kinetic war as opposed to a spy war. Therefore radical Islamic terrorism presented greater revenue generating potential, than China. And finally, just the shear ineptitude of the US intelligence community trying to find a true China hand in the intelligence community is a rarity to say the least. The intelligence community along with the rest of the US government are just plain ignorant when it comes to China.

Russian vs Ukraine

The Russian war with Ukraine is yet another example. The intel community had the American public convinced for decades that the Russian military was a threat to not only NATO but to America as well to drum up American public support for more defense spending. And once again the intel community proves to be inept and unethical. It is obvious that the Russian military is not only *not* a significant threat to NATO, it has even met considerable resistance against an underdeveloped and corrupt country like Ukraine.. Now they are doing the same thing with China to drum up American support for an American military intervention in Taiwan.

My view regarding Ukraine is like my view regarding Taiwan. These are not America's war, and we need to stay out of them. I have no ill will regarding either the Ukrainian or Taiwanese people; however, both of these conflicts are of internal sovereign matters with Russia and China. Furthermore, considering that the war in Ukraine is in Europe, it is time for America to let the Europeans handle their own security affairs. The Europeans are big boys with deep pockets; they are not children. They are fully capable of defending themselves. America has enough problems in America. During my time spent in the US Army, I realized that NATO is only in existence due to American

1. Funding
2. Military support (troops and equipment)
3. Political and military leadership

If America ceased supporting NATO, then NATO surely would cease to exist. So why is America still supporting NATO? The time has passed for the Europeans to take charge of Europe and to allow America to take care of Americans. There is no reason why the Europeans cannot build, maintain, and operate their own military security apparatus to protect Europeans. It is time for American taxpayer money to be spent on America-first initiatives.

Based on the US intelligence community's threat assessment on China, the current strategy toward China will not work. American politicians continually fail to see or act upon the viable solution as it would threaten their government careers. The truth is that American corporations and banks helped build China into what it is today. Unless America changes its own political course, it will not be able to compete with China. The solution to dealing with China is through the radical change of America's current political leadership system not with an offensive military operation. The following are quotes from US government agencies:

> "We consistently see that it's the Chinese government that poses the biggest long-term threat to our economic and national security."
>
> — FBI Director Christopher Wray at a joint appearance in MI5's London headquarters

> "The most important geopolitical threat we (America) face in the 21st century."
>
> — CIA Director William Burns called the Chinese government

> "China is a challenge to our (America) security, to our prosperity, to our values. The Peoples Republic of China is

coming ever closer to being a peer competitor in areas of relevance to national security and is pushing to revise global norms and institutions to its advantage, Haines added. They are challenging the United States in multiple arenas — economically, militarily and technologically."

— Avril Haines, the Director of National Intelligence

"China also remains a pacing threat and a major security challenge to the United States and its allies, he said. "Beijing has long viewed the United States as a strategic competitor, and China is capable of combining its economic, diplomatic, military and technological power to mount a sustained challenge to a stable and open international system."

— Army Lieutenant General Scott D. Berrier, Director of the Defense Intelligence Agency

"Let me talk a little bit about the strategic environment we see today. It does begin with China—that presents our greatest political challenge of our time," Nakasone explained. "This is not Cold War 2.0 and China is not the Soviet Union."

— U.S. Army General Paul M. Nakasone; Commander, U.S. Cyber Command; Director, National Security Agency

All these assessments are from the viewpoints of career government bureaucrats who are more interested in securing their careers than telling the hard truth about America's relationship with China. I have more operational knowledge and leadership perspective on China than probably anyone in the US government. Here is my risk assessment on China's threat to America:

> **China is the biggest *foreign* threat facing America's *hegemony*.**

Biggest Threat to America

China is *not* the biggest threat facing America. Furthermore, China threatens America's hegemony (specifically in Asia), but *not* America's survival. This is a frequently misunderstood point about China. Again, the overall biggest threat facing America is the continuous decline in the citizen's trust and support in the US government and US corporations. These two unethical and unpatriotic institutions are working in collaboration with each other to undermine the constitutional freedoms of American citizens as well as the national sovereignty of the United States. For the American system to survive, two distinct elements of our society must be changed, protected, increased, secured, promoted, honored, and aligned:

1. Constitutional rights and freedoms for all US citizens that allows them to live their private lives as they see fit.
2. Political and corporate patriotic nationalism that puts the interests of all US citizens and the country first.

The constitutional protections should be afforded to every American citizen and must be valued by being difficult to obtain. Through liberal immigration policies, the American government has undermined the freedoms, rights, and privileges of its citizens while at the same time haphazardly extending the sacred opportunity for foreigners to become US citizens. The American government needs to take into account these two mutually related facets of America:

1. **Protecting the rights of American citizens**: The FBI should not be allowed to spy on American Citizens without justifiable and reasonable probable cause; FISA should be abolished as it pertains to US Citizens. Without individual right to privacy, democracy will not survive.

1. **Placing a high value on American citizenship**: The US government must tighten immigration and naturalization requirements to reduce the number of foreigners being able to obtain US citizenship. If admission into America and the eventual procurement of US citizenship remains easy, then America will lose its sovereignty. The privilege of being an American citizen won't mean anything anymore.

The US government has too many lawyers and not enough leaders.

Senior US national security officials should be former military veterans. The directors of the FBI and CIA should be military veterans. There is no higher level of patriotism and loyalty to the country than military service. National security leaders who are military veterans are the nations most trusted citizens to lead the agencies that handle top secret information.

All national security agencies should be headed by veterans. It is time to stop putting bureaucrats in charge of national security. These government lawyers do not understand national security as they have never served in the military. If the security of America is compromised, it will be the US military who will have to answer the call. It will be military servicemembers called to the front lines to defend America.

A godless leader will lack the courage to enforce morality.

Morality vs Legality

This lack of ethical leadership within the US intelligence agencies was apparent during America's global war on terror—specifically with respect to the condoned torture of enemy combatants and prisoners of war, which was a complete and utter destruction of American values and respect for honor and dignity. From the torture of the prisoners in the Abu Ghraib Prison, to Guantanamo Bay, to the numerous covert black sites scattered across the globe where both CIA and FBI officers tortured supposed terrorists during "enhanced" interrogations, the security agencies went off the rails. Has America gone mad to justify this type of treatment on human beings?

The barbaric treatment of prisoners at the hands of US intelligence officers is a disgrace. Torture is never acceptable for a true leader. It is counter to what God intended for man. Killing another human being with dignity or purpose is a far cry from torturing a human being. During combat, killing is morally justified; it is facet in the Human Evolution of struggle and conflict. Regarding torture, this act transcends the notion of killing and is evil in nature. As a child, my father would take me hunting on many occasions, and he would always stress that prey animals should never have to suffer. The goal of a hunter is to kill the animal in the fastest and most painless way possible. A hunter should take pride in the hunt but should always respect and honor the kill. The overall purpose of being a hunter is not in the act of killing the animal but as a means to feed your family. Even the most despicable criminals on earth, such as child molesters and animal abusers, deserve to be punished or executed humanely. Should a person deserve to die, then they should die humanely. Torture should never be permitted.

How leaders in the US government could have condoned torture in the name of "protecting America" from terrorism is absolutely deplorable. US politicians should be ashamed of themselves for allowing torture to be committed by intelligence officers. When I hear about rumors, testimony, and evidence of China conducting live human organ harvesting, words cannot describe how I feel about this type of evil; however, leadership must first be established from the place of origin. Therefore, from America's perspective, discussions about human rights should first be examined from America's own actions, and the global war on terror has exposed America's awful lack of ethical concern for human beings.

Leadership focuses on morality as opposed to legality. Every human being deserves a dignified death, no matter what his or her background is or what crime he or she has committed. Even when execution may be the appropriate course of action, this person still deserves to die humanely and not be tortured. Furthermore, by condoning the use of torture, the US government will never rid itself of the immoral "residue" of its actions. The same moral compass that the American government uses in its treatment of foreign nationals on foreign soils may one day be equally and unethically used against US citizens, whether on American or foreign soil. When a government condones torture, it is a sign of the ending of a decaying empire.

The main reason for this vacuum in moral leadership has to do with weak men being in charge. What the government, media, academia, and corporations have dead wrong is their constant attack on masculinity as being toxic. This war against high testosterone alpha men is wrong and is destroying America. It allows unethical leaders to be in positions of power and leadership, especially in the government. Strong men make more ethical leaders than weak men do. Men who possess an enormous amount of courage are not afraid of the negative consequences of standing up for their moral beliefs—even if it means losing one's career. The reason why evil acts of torture were tolerated among the senior American government leaders was due to the fact that most of the men in power were weak and unwilling to stand their ground in the face of moral opposition from their superiors. Instead, they were willing to appease their bosses in exchange for job security. It is very dangerous to have weak men in leadership positions.

Philosophically speaking, good cannot exist without evil, meaning there will always be evil in human society. The best defense against evil is morally strong men in positions of leadership. Americans are witnessing this fact whether in the government or corporations. The leaders in both of these entities are supplanting their moral courage with egotistical survival and gain. Sooner or later a system like this will not survive as the men of courage and morality will no longer tolerate supporting such institutions and systems. America was founded by strong men with moral courage. Without these types of men in America, its collapse is definite.

We are all dead men walking.
Our time on earth will soon run its course.
Be brave and die with honor.

Right to Privacy

Evil men want to control people and to control people they need to know everything about them. That is why privacy is a such precious commodity and is essential toward free thought. If the citizens are not secure in their private affairs, then they will not feel comfortable or safe even in the privacy of their own homes. There are those who argue that if the citizens are doing nothing illegal, then they should not worry about any government surveillance into their private lives. Do you think the reverse would be true. If the government is not doing anything illegal, then the government should not be worried about the citizens knowing everything that happens within the government.

Privacy is something special. It is a unique trait to human beings and is essential to feel safe and free in conducting their affairs. Even if the citizen's private behaviors are absolutely legal, they are still vulnerable because where there is information, there is power.

Espionage is similar to prostitution.
Society will always have a demand for these activities.
Society will always attempt to conceal these activities.

Espionage is considered the second oldest profession. From the dawn of time, human beings have had an insatiable thirst for information—specifically secret and confidential information concerning other people, organizations, and governments. From government intelligence agencies to media news outlets to business firms to your nosy next-door neighbor to your girlfriend who is suspicious of infidelity, human beings have an unquenchable thirst for privileged information. Information or intelligence is power, and the more private or secretive this information remains, the greater advantage those who are able to surreptitiously procure it will have. Americans must never surrender their privacy to the government, or to any other entities demanding their private information, including employers, technology firms, or media.

> **If we are going to live in a democracy, the bulk of power needs to be with the people. Whoever has the data has the power.**

Privacy is also the problem when it comes to law enforcement. When a police officer questions a citizen, regardless of whether or not they have committed a crime, they should respect the citizen's right to remain silent. Law enforcement officers frequently and intentionally choose to forget and ignore this civil right. Remaining silent is *not* an admission of guilt, but a constitutional right the police are sworn to uphold.

When I was illegally interrogated by Customers and Border Patrol agents at the O'Hare airport, they failed to honor my repeated requests to remain silent. During my time in the FBI, I had witnessed this behavior time and time again. Almost every time a suspect chose to remain silent, the police would assume that this was an admission of guilt or suspicious behavior. The police would continue to harass the citizen in order to provoke or intimidate the suspect into speaking. This was exactly what they did to me at O'Hare. The CBP agents accused me of trying to hide something. They felt it was fully in their right to interrogate me despite my repeated requests to remain silent. This behavior is absolutely unconstitutional and unethical. As a veteran, I fought to defend these very rights that I chose to exercise. I have no interest in telling anybody my private information, especially to law enforcement. I prefer to keep my business to myself as my private affairs are just that *private*. Today's law enforcement exhibit such an arrogant and domineering behavior. Citizens need no reason whatsoever to justify their decision to remain silent when dealing with the police. If a citizen wishes to have his or her personal information remain private, then law enforcement should immediately and professionally honor their requests; it is as simple as that.

During my time in the FBI, I conducted wiretaps, listening in on my target's phone conversations. As dictated by law, the scope and purpose of the wiretap was to only listen in on anything that the target was discussing that related to criminal or intelligence activity. All personal conversations were required to be minimized; therefore, FBI agents should not be listening in on the target's private conversations that were of non-criminal or non-intelligence matters, such as conversations about their marriage, sexual behaviors, infidelity, medical problems, health conditions, hobbies, interests, children, politics, racist views, family, psychological problems, fears, and more. This minimization rule was frequently overlooked and not enforced, especially with respect to national security operations, as almost any and all information regarding the target can be justified as intelligence. What is even more disturbing is how many agents found it entertaining to eavesdrop on the private matters of their targets (including US citizens) and then joke about them with other agents in an unprofessional manner. It's not that FBI agents are any more curious or nosy than other Americans. Most people are into knowing about and talking about other people's private affairs; this is a common vice, hence the popularity of talk shows, gossip reports, tabloids, reality TV. That is why protecting the privacy of US Citizens is of the utmost importance. American Citizens should do everything possible to keep the American government out of their homes and to keep American citizens' private affairs private.

The sanctity of privacy is the sanctity of human rights.
American citizens have a right to be secure in their private affairs.

I am quite aware of the vulnerability and damages caused by the government's unethical spying on innocent citizens. The FBI spied on me during my time both inside and outside the FBI, both domestically and overseas. Their illegal and immoral spy campaign elevated to the level that they colluded with other countries' foreign intelligence agencies to spy on me while I lived overseas, thus threatening my personal safety. I was not involved in any illegal activity, and the FBI surely did not have any evidence of probable cause of a crime; therefore, I should have been entitled to the full legal due process and all the constitutional protections before the FBI spied on me and my relationships, emails, communications, financial transactions, locations, and even what I did in my own home. When a person is spied on, it makes them feel vulnerable, scared, paranoid, angry, betrayed, demoralized, insulted, and alone. Of course, being spied on by a foreign intelligence agency comes with the territory, but I am specifically referring to being spied on by your own government, the American government.

When I left the FBI, this spy campaign against me continued, and it is still ongoing. The FBI's vindictive investigation to destroy me has not been able to undercover any evidence, because I have never committed any crimes. Therefore, their hatred against me is targeted against my conservative political views. Their entire spy investigation against me is a complete unethical political witch hunt. When I was in Chicago, the FBI had a surveillance team on me. Not only was the FBI stalking me in Chicago, but when I discovered their surveillance, the angry and surprised FBI operative physically assaulted me, as documented in chapter 4. This is just absolutely absurd and also criminal. What kind of country has the USA become, when foreigners, refugees, and immigrants (legal or illegal) are welcomed, but a military veteran is assaulted by his very own government. The FBI didn't just tarnish my reputation; it also communicated with foreign governments to gain information about me and in the process endangered my life and ruined my career, yet again. This is the textbook example of a tyrannical government that not only destroys the life of a citizen but a military veteran. What kind of government has the United States turned into?

Speechless is the best way I can describe my feelings as I write this book and reflect on how unethical and illegal the FBI's actions have been. I also know that I am not alone, that countless other innocent citizens are also being unconstitutionally spied upon by the government, regardless of whether there is any probable cause of criminal activity present or not. A corrupt system like this cannot last.

In 2010, I had already left the United States due to how this corruption was affecting my life. Even now, despite me having left

America, the US government's authoritarian treatment is still persecuting me. If US citizens do not stand up to the overreaching unethical government and demand their civil rights, then soon there will be nothing left to stand for. That is why I'm writing this book. I had never wanted to take my case public; I have always valued my privacy and the ethos of being a Quiet Professional. However, the FBI has pushed me too far. They have refused to speak with me as well as the Inspector General of the DOJ, and even the politicians have ignored me, so I am left me with no other choice but to take a public stand and expose the American globalist government and American globalist corporations. They have spit in the face of patriotic American military veterans. Unless something drastically changes, the American dream will die forever and thus be laid to rest in the US military cemeteries where the souls of our American patriotic forefathers who fought and died to keep that dream alive are laid. May God pass judgement upon America and may the judgement be final.

> **Few men have the virtue to withstand the highest bidder.**
> **—George Washington**

10

China Is Not the Enemy: My China Journey

When I was a cadet at West Point, I formally began my path to become a China Hand. Since childhood, I had already been fully immersing myself in learning about China, specifically Chinese boxing （咏春）, Chinese philosophy （道教）, and Chinese medicine （中医）.[1] As a young child around eight years old my father took me to New York City's Chinatown for lunch. He nor anyone in my family ever had any special interest in China other than enjoying the occasional Chinese cuisine. As my father drove into Chinatown, I remember looking out of the car window and thinking that I was in a foreign country. When we arrived at the Chinese restaurant, I was awestruck at seeing and hearing all the strange sights and noises. I can still picture the roasted ducks hanging by the skillets (北京烤鸭)[2] in the windows of the restaurants. All the Chinese characters written everywhere—on the menu, on the walls, on signs—captured my attention. I was enamored by these strange symbols. I asked my father what the writing meant; he just laughed at me saying, "I have no clue, why don't you learn what it means." I could not wait to begin learning the Chinese language. Unfortunately, both my public high school and MMI did not offer Chinese language instruction, so it was not until I entered West Point that I was given the chance to formally begin studying Mandarin Chinese, and of course I jumped at the opportunity.

Years later, when I was working in the US intelligence community, I continued my pursuit of China by enrolling in a graduate-level Chinese studies program at the University of San Francisco. This opportunity allowed me to delve further into the comprehensive study of China with respect to the language, culture, history, politics, economics, philosophy, and most important to understand China from a leadership perspective. Despite the US government and media trying to convince the American people that China is the enemy, all one has to do is look at how the American globalist corporations view China, and it is easy to see that China is not the enemy. In fact, it is a strategic international business partner. I am not saying that China is an ally or friend to America, but more accurately, China rests in the gray area of being both a ruthless competitor and a strategic partner.

The biggest threat to America is liberalism, feminism, globalism, rampant immigration, multiculturalism, diversity, and corporate greed.

Yes, it is indeed true that China wants to supplant America as the hegemony of Asia. However, as America's globalist empire continues to police the world, it prevents any nation from rising in power and threatening its top post as the world's leader. The problem is that America (the government and corporations) feels threatened by any country who wishes to topple America's global dominance. While the typical American is fooled into to worrying about the supposed threat of China, the FBI batters down the doors of American citizens with search warrants in order to confiscate all of your private possessions in their unethical witch hunt to find anti-government material. Then the FBI builds its case to eventually arrest you on charges of domestic terrorism. It is the American government and corporations who the American people should be truly afraid of, as these two entities are working in unison to accomplish their diabolic plan:

Remove freedom-loving American patriots and replace them with socialist-loving globalist liberals.

If China truly were the enemy, then why wouldn't the US government deny all Chinese citizens from obtaining visas to America and thus denying them the ability to immigrate to America. Of course, the US government will say that the Chinese people are not the enemy; it is only the Chinese government that is the threat. If this is true, then why are American Corporations comfortable and agreeable in doing business directly with the Chinese Government in China, which is the standard norm for doing business in China. If China truly is the enemy, then why would American corporations be so willing and anxious to do business with the Chinese government; obviously money is the answer. Here's a key difference between American corporations and Chinese corporations:

> **Chinese corporations** are required to ensure that whatever product or service they provide to either China or the world, results in direct benefit to China and the Chinese people.

American Corporations are not required to have any type of loyalty or patriotism to America or the American people; they are allowed to be as greedy and as globalist as they want.

In 2010; I left America, because I did not want to live in the godless globalist America anymore. I knew that the American system was destined for collapse. I moved to China because it would cement my lifelong goal of becoming a China expert. When I was in the FBI, I repeatedly warned FBI management that China was by far the bigger threat to America than radical Islamic terrorism. They did not believe me or fully understand China, and I don't think most ever will. Despite my departure from America, however, the FBI's global tentacles refused to let me go, as their unlawful and immoral spy campaign against me continued unabated.

It is time for American Patriots to wake up and realize that the real enemy is not from some foreign country located halfway across the globe. The real enemy is the one who is just a "knock on your door" away. The real enemy is the one who controls your life through unpatriotic laws and controls your money through repressive taxes. The real enemy is the one who ceases to honor the men and women of the armed forces. The real enemy wishes to replace patriotic nationalism with liberal globalism. The real enemy wants to erase your history and label your forefathers as evil. The real enemy wants to shut down your voice and force you to comply with liberal ideology. The real enemy wants to turn masculine men into submissive slaves. The real enemy wants to turn you away from Judeo-Christianity and force you to embrace atheist Marxism. The real enemy wants to deny women the joy of motherhood and compel them into a life of corporate servitude. The real enemy punishes you for being proud of your God-inherited identity and compels you to despise who you are. The real enemy forces you to accept that your home is welcome to the whole world whether you like it or not. The real enemy sends you to jail or censures you for speaking your opinion. The real enemy sees America as evil and racist. The real enemy put profits before its citizens. The real enemy does not care about the birthrate of the country as they view Americans as replaceable through mass immigration. The real enemy will force you to eat insects and soybeans while they eat meat and dairy. The real enemy will force you to use environmentally friendly public transportation while they fly around the world on their private jets. The real enemy will destroy local private capitalism and force you to only buy their corporate globalist products. The real enemy will replace the American worker with anyone and anywhere who is more cost effective.

To know your enemy, you must become your enemy.

—Sun Wu, *The Art of War*

（孙武，[3] 孙子兵法）[4]

China has a collective attitude that puts the group, the family, and the nation before the individual. They are more singularly oriented as opposed to America's diversity of cultures. No matter how long I live in China, I will never be accepted as Chinese since I am not ethnically Chinese. All foreigners will remain "guests" in China. No matter how long they stay, China will never be their home. For example, an ethnically Chinese person who is born and grows up in another country and moves to China later in life will be accepted as Chinese and will be given the opportunity to obtain Chinese citizenship—if they are willing to give up their current citizenship. China will always be home to ethnically Chinese people regardless of whether or not they are living in China or abroad; however, will America always be home to Americans, especially if everyone in this world can become an American citizen? What exactly is an American? This question alone will cause much anxiety and stress in the politically correct liberal world. China is stable because they are similar. America is unstable because we are diverse. The more Americans embrace the fools dream of "diversity is our strength," the closer to collapse America will be.

There is no greater evil in this world than genocide.

Genocide

Allow me to begin my balanced perspective with the immediate high-level tension points between China and America. As a proud Jew, the mere word *genocide* triggers thoughts of the WWII holocaust. Many Americans point to the genocide being committed in China's Xinjiang （ 新疆 ） [5] region regarding the Chinese ethnic minority group the Uyghurs （ 维吾尔族 ） .[6] I have personally visited this region on three separate occasions and have also personally spoken with many of the local Uyghurs about their lives in China. Overall, I have concluded that a form of genocide is indeed being imposed by the Chinese government on this ethnic minority group. It pains me to see and hear what is happening to the Uyghurs, and I urge the Chinese government to find a humanitarian solution to the problem as soon as possible because there is indeed a problem on both sides of the issue. There is violence from the side of the Uyghurs, who have been responsible for numerous acts of domestic terrorism in China. It is true that much domestic terrorism in China can be sourced to the violent extremism of the Uyghur people. However, committing genocide is clearly not the answer. When I evaluate the genocide that is being committed in Xinjiang, I am reminded of the leadership principle based on judgement:

> **Everyone is entitled to freely and openly judge anyone. However, before one judges others, one should first judge themself.**

With this leadership principle in mind, before Western nations condemn China for genocide, they must first evaluate their own actions properly.

Before I talk about America, let me address Israel's treatment of the Palestinians. As a Jew, I am naturally biased toward the Jewish people and the state of Israel. I am a proud Zionist, just as I am a proud American nationalist. The Jewish people absolutely deserve a country where they can call their home and a country where they can feel safe as a people, a Jewish state. Therefore, I emphatically state: God bless and protect Israel. However, with all that said, I have lost many of my good Jewish friends due to my views regarding the treatment of the Palestinians. The treatment of the Palestinians in Israel can be described at the very least as a form of apartheid. Now, I'm no Middle East expert and don't have any solutions to this problem, but I humbly ask for the Israeli government to strive to work toward a peaceful solution with the Palestinians while maintaining a steadfast devotion to securing the Jewish state of Israel for the Jewish people. The humanitarian conditions of the Palestinian people need to be improved to an acceptable international standard which leaves no guilt on the faces of Zionist Jews like myself. Perhaps the two-state solution is indeed the best and necessary course of action after all. Because I am a nationalist at heart, I truly believe that most of the time the best solution for two distinct and incompatible groups of people is separation.

Good Fences make good neighbors.

When I was a new agent trainee (NAT) at the FBI Academy, we took a trip to the US Holocaust Memorial Museum in Washington, DC, to educate and remind the soon to be new FBI agents about the horrors in world history when governments lose their moral compass. Even though I think the trip remembering the horrors of what happens when weak men fail to stand up to evil and is indeed a valuable tool in teaching moral leadership—and the Jewish Holocaust is a prime example of that—something however seemed strangely inadequate with that educational trip. I wondered why there was no field trip to an American Indian Genocide Museum as that trip would have been even more important since the genocide that the Native Americans suffered was committed by our very own government on American soil. It just seemed odd to me that American government men were learning about genocide atrocities committed by the German government when there were genocide atrocities committed by our very own government in America.

If one were to prioritize which museum FBI NATs should attend, I would think the American Indian Genocide Museum would take priority. Of course, having the FBI NATs learn about both genocides would have been even better. I certainly felt no guilt when I visited the Jewish Holocaust museum, and I am sure many of my fellow FBI NATs felt that same way because none of us were responsible for the Jewish genocide, and it took place on an entirely different continent under the authority of a different government. Learning about the Native American genocide, however, would have been different. The FBI should feel guilty for what the American government did to the Native Americans on American soil. What is even more shocking is that the Native American genocide is estimated by some researchers to have killed well over 10 million people. One would think Americans would prioritize the Native American genocide over the Jewish genocide.

Before Americans have the gall to criticize China, they should first make amends for the genocide that occurred in America to the Native Americans under the rule of the American government. During my time spent in Germany, I witnessed how they taught all students about the Jewish Holocaust with such intensity so as to instill a perpetual lifelong guilt in the permanent psyche of every German. While growing up in America, on the other hand, students are not educated in any form about the Native American genocide or taught to have any guilt toward the subject. American globalist corporations, such as my former unethical employers Boeing and Amazon, have business operations in Xinjiang. In fact, I took business trips to Boeing and Amazon's Xinjiang operations and witnessed the situation with the Uyghurs in the region there. If America truly condemns China for the genocide in Xinjiang, then the government should condemn American corporations for operating in Xinjiang. These greedy American globalist corporations do not care about the lives of the Uyghurs. In fact, these globalist corporations really do not have any high or lofty moral codes. Their ultimate purpose is to serve the financial interests of their shareholders. So again, the American government should first condemn American corporations doing business in Xinjiang and then own up to its part in the cruel history of the Native American genocide before it judges the Chinese government with regard to Xinjiang.

Judging others is justified, and it is human nature; however, before you judge others, first ensure that you have properly judged yourself.

The War Machine

There are so many war hawks in America constantly scaring the American Public by overstating the military threat from China. They say how America needs to be ready to go to war with China and particularly be ready to defend Taiwan. These people are part of the military-industrial complex. First off, the military threat from China is vastly overstated. Remember how the unethical and incompetent US intelligence community predicted that the Russian military is a threat to NATO. Yet now people from all over the world have witnessed that Russia cannot even defeat the less-than-modern country of Ukraine, let alone a modern military force like NATO.

The US intelligence community is at it again (remember weapons of mass destruction in Iraq) as they beat the war drums against China in the hopes of spurring America into war thus keeping the taxpayer profit streams pouring into the stocks and pockets of the American globalist defense corporations. I have witnessed firsthand the Chinese military, and it does not pose any credible threat to America. However, in the Asian Pacific, the US military does pose a threat to China. China is the one who is scared, not America. That is why the Chinese feel a much stronger nationalist fever than Americans. The Chinese government is afraid of an American military invasion or confrontation. It is very true, however, that the Chinese military continues to get stronger year by year, and it needs to be watched very closely by US intelligence. Within twenty or more years, I may perhaps change my mind about China's military strength versus the American military. Regarding China's primary national security concerns, however, China is in fact more worried about their domestic issues than foreign threats like America. The Chinese government throws the bulk of its resources toward maintaining domestic stability in a country that is seeing an ever increase in domestic challenges in the form of:

1. Covid pandemic and the draconian zero-Covid lockdown policy
2. Record-low birth Rates causing serious population decline
3. Continued conflict with Hong Kong regarding cultural and legal unification
4. Growing tensions with local citizens' demand for human rights
5. Continued internal tensions in the Xinjiang and Tibet regions
6. Growing fever and strength regarding Taiwan's rejection of China
7. Domestic food and energy scarcity and dependence on foreign supply

8. Increasing health concerns due to pollution from environmental degradation
9. Decreased Western foreign investment and business partnerships
10. Increase of domestic capital flight and citizen emigration

Taiwan and Racism

Regarding a military confrontation, the biggest hotspot between China and America is Taiwan. It is no secret that China considers Taiwan part of its sovereign territory and will utilize maximum military force to retake ownership of the Taiwanese province if necessary. If America enters the military fray in defending Taiwan from a Chinese invasion, I'm certain Beijing would not hesitate to use nuclear weapons in its efforts to defend its territorial integrity, which would include Taiwan. Do the American people really want to risk a nuclear war with China over sovereignty of Taiwan?

Besides the typical profit incentives which would motivate the American military-industrial complex to wage war with China over Taiwan, what are the true benefits of this war to the normal, everyday American citizens should America defend Taiwan. I have visited Taiwan on numerous occasions and can adamantly state that it is a splendid country with an overall superior quality of life to that of mainland China. In fact, the quality of life in Taiwan is so good that it can sometimes even rival the standards found in many Western countries. Despite the fact that Taiwan is an excellent democratic country, that fact alone does not qualify Taiwan as a country that the American people must defend by military means and thus put the American people at risk and also the taxpayer under a huge burden.

Even though the Taiwanese government and people are very cultured and friendly, they too exhibit the same typical racist thinking that is so apparent outside of Western countries. How many ethnically non-Asian Taiwanese citizens have you ever met? It is almost impossible for a non-ethnic Chinese person to obtain Taiwanese citizenship. Furthermore, the Taiwanese government grants dual citizenship only to its native Taiwanese citizens. Any foreigner seeking to obtain Taiwanese citizenship through naturalization must renounce their previous citizenship as a rule of law. Furthermore, even those non-ethnic Asian foreigners who are able to become a Taiwanese citizen will experience racism from the vast majority of local Taiwanese citizens who will not accept the full integration of these non-Asian foreigners into their society despite their holding Taiwanese citizenship. This racism includes limited job opportunities and societal marginalization Citizens. Ninety-nine percent of Taiwanese are ethnically Chinese. To even find a non-Chinese Taiwanese citizen is next to impossible. So the question again is: Why would the American globalist government and American globalist corporations who constantly tout the importance of diversity, equity, and inclusion want to defend a racist country like Taiwan? Again, I have met many Taiwanese People and I think they are friendly and kind, and I still think Taiwan is an extraordinary country; however, if we as Americans are going to evaluate Taiwan based on Western liberal standards, then Taiwan is an extremely racist country. Why should American Military Service members go to war to defend Taiwan and thus give their lives for a country that would then discriminate against them should they ever want to live in Taiwan after the war? If Americans knew just how racist Taiwan is, they would change their views on giving their hard-earned tax dollars and risk the lives of American soldiers to defend Taiwan.

On a similar note, my advice to former presidential candidate Andrew Yang, who is a Taiwanese-American: Dear Andrew, before you talk about the racism that you have experienced in America due to your Asian ethnicity, I urge you to first look at the racism that is present in Taiwan with respect to non-Asians. You have had an extraordinary opportunity granted to you in America. You got to run for the office of the President of the United States. Many Asian-Americans are successful politicians in America. I kindly ask you to ask yourself how many non-Asian politicians are represented in Taiwan. How many non-Asian political, military, and business leaders are there in Taiwan? I totally support you for being proud of your Asian identity, as well as being proud of your Taiwanese roots. I believe Taiwan is an extraordinary country; however, it is also an extremely racist country. Therefore, before you criticize the over-hyped racism in America, please first evaluate the extreme racism found in Taiwan. And to all the readers, I want to reemphasize:

There is no other country in the world that treats women, racial minorities, and immigrants better than America.

America is actually the Least Racist Country in the World

Nationalism

Also, I want to be very clear when I speak about the racist cultures of China and Taiwan. First, I am not singling out these two countries by any means. Almost all non-Western countries in the world share the same racist attitudes as China and Taiwan. Second, please do not confuse my sentiment on "racist culture" as being evil or bad. Even though the word *racist* is a prerogative, I actually support the immigration and citizenship policies of these non-Western countries. Again, I am in no way, angry or bitter at the idea that China has never granted me or any other non-Chinese person citizenship, or even rarely offers non-Chinese permanent residence. Again, China is not my country, and the Chinese government has 100 percent the legal and moral authority to decide who can become a citizen or permanent residence in their country. I am a supporter of nationalism and believe that liberal immigration policies (as found in America and the West) are a grave national security threat for its citizens and the next generations who will eventually become the minority.

Although, I fully support non-Western nations conservative and nationalistic approach to immigration, I have a problem with two things:

1. Non-Western countries, including China, calling America a racist country. When I see on the news that non-Western countries label or condemn America for being racist or Xenophobic, I find it both hilarious and insulting. My advice to China's media propaganda machine is to quickly and sternly change your strategic messaging with regard to this subject for two reasons: First, more and more Americans are discovering the truth about non-Western countries' racist policies toward foreigners; therefore, Americans will view this

type of non-Western propaganda as bigoted deceit and the result will be more distrust toward China. Second, it would be better to show your own Chinese citizens all the violence, chaos, and disunity found in America as a tool to justify to your own people why China should never adopt the liberal globalist immigration policies of America but should continue with your nationalist approach to immigration.

2. Reciprocity. This issue is with my government not enforcing a basic reciprocity measure. I would expect the American government to adopt either these same nationalist immigration policies as found in non-Western countries, thus severely reducing foreign immigration or just enforce simple reciprocity laws. If Americans cannot become citizens in these non-Western countries, then these non-Western immigrants cannot become American citizens. This follows the simple leadership principle of fairness.

I am a proud nationalist, and as such, I believe every country on earth should be given the freedom for self-determination. Of course, there will be international tensions; however, we as a global community must work together and allow every nation on earth to have its own right to self-governance. Therefore, I look at issues facing China as issues that China must deal with, and American intervention is not the answer. This includes Taiwan, Hong Kong, Tibet, Xinjiang, and the South China Sea. China should be left alone to deal with its own issues; and this same philosophy should apply to all nations. However, I am also a champion of free speech, and therefore, just because I am against American military intervention does not mean I am against the right for any nation in the world to be able to speak out on whatever issues they want—commending or condemning other countries for their actions or policies.

As a former military officer, I am not naive to think that military intervention is never an option. Throughout history war has been a part of mankind, and it will probably always be that way; however, the key is for nations to make war a last resort. America has certainly not been a good example of this philosophy. America is the only country in the world to have used nuclear weapons in war.

Regarding the South China Sea, many argue that this region falls outside China's territory and therefore "nationalist theory" does not apply here as the sea encompasses multiple nations. China declares it belongs to them, and other nations should not interfere. I partially agree. My stance is that the sea certainly does not belong to the United States; therefore, should America want to intervene, it should only intervene at the behest of its allies in the Asian region who have a direct territorial claim on the South China Sea. America should work through, by, and with its Asian allies in the region as opposed to taking any unilateral military or political actions. Should an Asian country who has a direct claim to the South China Sea ask America for assistance— and it is in the best interest of the American *people,* as opposed to corporations to assist this Asian nation—then America should work at the behest of this allied Asian country to help resolve the South China Sea conflict.

At the end of the day, the America people are going to have to ask themselves: how are these foreign wars or interventions actually helping out America. Sooner or later, the American military-industrial complex will no longer have the funding or the volunteers necessary to continue their campaign of dominance. Sooner or later, the American empire will run out of blood and treasure to support the imperialism of never-ending wars.

If his forces are united, separate them.

—**Sun Wu, The Art of War** （孙武，孙子兵法）

Corporate Capitalism: Un-Patriotic and Un-American

American corporations have supplanted patriotism with greed. They are globalists whose primary loyalty is to their corporate shareholders. For example, the Boeing Company, an official member of the military-industrial complex pretends to rally behind the American flag, the American military, and the American people. It portrays itself as a patriotic American company; however, at the same time, China is Boeing's largest overseas partner. I worked for Boeing in Beijing, China, as the regional security crisis advisor for greater China. In fact, during my time with Boeing, I was part of its largest single foreign investment in the entire history of Boeing: a $700-plus million factory in Zhoushan (舟山),[1] China.

Boeing

Boeing plays both sides. Boeing convinces the American government that China is a military threat, so the government will buy more Boeing defense products. At the same time, Boeing partners with the Chinese government in order to persuade China to buy more Boeing airplanes. Globalists have no loyalty to any single nation or people; they are only loyal to their global corporate shareholders.

More than one-third of Boeing's revenues come from the US government. In fact, the US government, and by default, the American taxpayer, is the single largest customer for Boeing. Boeing is a quasi-governmental agency; therefore, one would think that Boeing, unlike other corporations, should have a higher standard of patriotism and loyalty to US citizens since the bulk of their profits come straight from the pocket of US taxpayers. This is such an obvious unethical conflict of interest:

1. The Boeing Company reaps huge amounts of revenues from the US government (meaning US taxpayers) by supplying defense products in order to defend against evil China.
2. The Boeing Company reaps huge amounts of revenues from the Chinese government by helping China become a more modernized and stronger country.

During my time with Boeing, one of my colleagues, Doug, was a former US Marine Corps officer who was assigned to another Asian country. We both witnessed unethical discriminatory behavior on the part of Boeing management in Asia that was being condoned by Boeing management at Headquarters (HQ) in Seattle, Washington. In the summer of 2016, we both filed Equal Employment Opportunity (EEO) discrimination complaints against both Boeing Asia and Boeing HQ. Following our complaints, Boeing American management from HQ retaliated against both of us. They threatened our job security and made our work conditions a hostile environment, to which both Doug and I filed additional hostile work environment complaints to Boeing HQ. I immediately procured a lawyer in the United States to prepare to take legal action against Boeing, as both Doug and I knew, Boeing would retaliate against anyone they viewed as a threat or liability as a result of this discrimination complaint. In January 2017, Doug was pushed out of Boeing and left with ill feelings. At the same time, our initial manager, who Doug and I accused of discrimination and who was an Indian national, was also pushed out of Boeing. I knew I was next, and in February 2017, I was at the Hilton Hotel in Zhoushan, China. One of the maids accused me of sexual harassment. Boeing management immediately launched an internal investigation. The exact same investigator from Boeing HQ who handled my EEO discrimination complaints (and subsequently informed me that all of my complaints lacked evidence, therefore they were all unsubstantiated) was now going to investigate me for alleged sexual misconduct with the Chinese maid. I told my lawyer that Boeing was going to use this false charge of sexual misconduct as a pretext to terminate my employment. I had no faith that Boeing was going to do an ethical or unbiased investigation into this matter, so I formally requested Boeing Management get the Chinese police involvement in the case. Boeing refused, and a month later I was terminated from Boeing. And just like my Marine Corps colleague, Boeing replaced both of us with foreign nationals—in my case, with a Chinese national.

Determined to seek justice, I decided to sue Boeing not only in America but also in China. When I first met with my Chinese lawyer in Beijing, he was completely shocked on how could Boeing terminate me over these baseless sexual allegations that did not even happen on Boeing property or even involve any Boeing employees. I informed him that this was a retaliatory measure due to my previous EEO complaints against Boeing management. He told me that in China, a Chinese company would never terminate their employee over a matter such as this. Because there was no evidence, the company should have taken the side of their trusted employee as opposed to taking the side of an unknown stranger who is not even associated with the company.

Despite no evidence, Boeing had decided to disregard my testimony in their internal investigation—even though I am a US citizen, military veteran, former US intelligence officer, and employee in good standing with the Boeing for approximately two years. I was what they call a "known quantity" to Boeing. My accuser (the Hilton Hotel maid) on the other hand was an "unknown quantity"; Boeing had no idea who she was, other than the fact that she was a Chinese citizen who worked for the hotel. Despite all of this, Boeing decided to trust and believe a Chinese national over me, despite no evidence to support her claims.

Disloyal and unpatriotic Boeing sided with a Chinese citizen over an American citizen.

Disloyal and unpatriotic American corporations also side with China over America.

Lawsuit in China

During the trial in Beijing, the Chinese judge was amazed at the fact that Boeing did not honor my repeated requests to have Chinese police involvement. He specifically asked Boeing why they disregarded my multiple requests for police involvement. Boeing responded that the hotel maid, the Hilton Hotel management, and Boeing management all unanimously preferred not to have any police involvement as they all did not want to have any adverse influences. Boeing cared more about the reputations of a non-Boeing employee (the maid) and two multinational companies than on their very own employee (myself). Boeing specifically did not honor my request for police involvement because they very well knew that the Chinese police would immediately see that I was the innocent party and that Boeing's real motive was not in the pursuit of truth and justice but was actually to terminate me by whatever means possible in retaliation for my EEO complaints. The Chinese court ultimately sided with me and ruled that Boeing's unilateral decision to terminate me violated Chinese labor law. Since Boeing was unable to provide any evidence, it was illegal for Boeing to terminate my employment contract with them.

As I reflect on my personal experience with the Chinese justice system, I think about the state of America, where female privilege is all too present in the legal system. I told my Chinese lawyer about the justice system in America regarding sexual allegations, and he was shocked. "I thought America's legal system was based upon evidence," he commented. This is clearly not the case for any sexual allegations that women make against men in America. To all American men, never be ignorant of the fact that a woman in America can accuse you of rape, sexual harassment, sexual assault, sexual discrimination, or anything sexual or gender related without any evidence, and you as a man will still suffer major consequences or even be convicted—even if you are innocent. In America, when it comes to allegations of sexual misconduct, a man is considered guilty until proven innocent.

I was terminated from my job by the unethical Boeing management; however, I am so thankful that the Chinese legal system delivered me justice. It's a shame that as an American veteran, I had to depend on the Chinese courts in order to get a fair and just trial from the unethical American Boeing corporation. What an absolute farce

the Boeing Corporation has become. Unethical behavior on part of
Boeing is nothing new:

> Boeing and its former CEO Dennis Muilenburg agreed to pay
> hefty fines to settle charges from the Securities and Exchange
> Commission that they misled the public about the safety of the
> 737 Max following two <u>fatal crashes</u> in 2018 and 2019.[2]

After the trial, Boeing attempted to negotiate a settlement with me
on condition that I drop my pending lawsuit against them in the United
States. I declined their offer as I was determined to seek justice as an
ethical whistleblower. No US citizen or veteran should ever have to
experience the immoral conduct on the part of globalist American
management. Their greed for profits has left them without any moral
compass or sense of duty and loyalty to America, American citizens,
and especially military veterans. Also, do not be fooled to think that
the Boeing Corporation really ever cared about this Chinese hotel
maid. Boeing just used her like a pawn to terminate me. Before the
Chinese court hearing took place, the hotel maid was terminated from
her job due to misconduct; Boeing never had any care or concern for
her well-being; she was merely a tool used by Boeing to get rid of me.
To the American Hilton Hotel corporation, your globalist greed has
also impaired your moral values. Your management has failed in their
responsibility to ensure its customers (me) are treated with dignity and
safety. As a guest who was staying at your hotel during this incident, I
specifically requested the Chinese police involvement into the
unethical and illegal actions of one of your employees (the hotel maid);
however, your hotel management did not honor my request. They
instead honored Boeing's request of no police involvement. This was,
of course, due to Boeing and your hotel signing a significant long-term,
multi-million-dollar business contract together as Boeing planned to

utilize your hotel for long-term expat housing. Your hotel management did not want to jeopardize the lucrative business deal. As a globalist corporation, your actions displayed an unethical concern for truth and justice. I suggest you reevaluate your company's substandard values.

To David Calhoun, the president and chief executive officer of The Boeing Company, Dave Komendat, vice president and chief security officer, and Timothy Lynch, HR Director for Asia, gentlemen, your own Boeing values statement states:

> Lead on safety, quality, **integrity** and sustainability: In everything we do and in all aspects of our business, we will make safety our top priority, strive for first-time quality, **hold ourselves to the highest ethical standards**, and continue to support a sustainable future.[3] (emphasis added)

All of you have failed to honor your company's values by tolerating unethical actions of discrimination, promoting a hostile work environment, and retaliating against me for reporting ethical problems. None of you have ever served in the military, so I do not expect you to fully understand the concepts of patriotism, honor, and loyalty to America.

In my case alone, despite any evidence, you and your management believed the testimony of an unknown Chinese citizen over me, an American veteran and your employee. Therefore, it should be of no surprise that Americans do not believe any of you, or any Boeing senior manager. Your unethical actions were done in retaliation to my EEO complaints against you and your management.

Boeing needs to rectify its immoral and unpatriotic management behavior. Therefore, my leadership assignment for you, should you accept it, is to reevaluate Boeing's relationship with the American people. What is your oath of loyalty to America and its citizens? That is the primary question to ponder. Furthermore, I recommend each of you seek leadership counseling from your religious, philosophical, or spiritual advisor and request forgiveness. God will forgive; he forgives all who repent. If you do so, I will forgive both of you too, as God wills.

Lawsuit in America

Regarding my lawsuit in America, Boeing hired a top tier global law firm. Their strategy was to never allow my case to go to trial because they knew they would lose. Therefore, they petitioned the presiding judge to get my case dismissed on various grounds. The back-and-forth attempts by Boeing's legal team to get my case thrown out went along for three years, and I had to spend well over 75,000 USD in legal fees. Considering I was unemployed throughout much of this time, the financial burden was causing serious stress and depression. As I continued to demand a trial, Boeing's defense team continued to file petitions for various reasons to cause delays. Finally, at the three-year mark, Judge Rebecca Ruth Pallmeyer, chief United States district Judge of the United States District Court of the Northern District of Illinois, sided with Boeing and ruled to not allow my case to go to court. The judge dismissed the entire case in favor of Boeing. I was utterly shocked. Unlike my exceptional Chinese lawyer, my American lawyer (Jonathan Goldman[4]) was both incompetent and negligent. Both in my EEO complaints to Boeing and also in my formal dialogue with my lawyer, Mr. Goldman. I specifically stated that the straw that broke the camel's back in terms of my desire to sue Boeing was the reckless violation of my private medical information being negatively discussed among Boeing management. My medical injuries, which resulted in part due to my military service, were sensitive and private, and I demanded they be kept private.

Despite my repeated requests for Medical Privacy, following Judge Pallmeyer's verdict, the internet came alive with numerous articles saying the reason why Boeing terminated me was because I was a sexual predator, and included the open publication of my private medical information. I was astounded, no one ever warned me that my case information, including my private medical information, would eventually be published on the internet for public consumption. This is how a whistleblower is treated by the American Legal system? I had to battle with numerous internet sites to get my information taken down, yet there are still sites up to this day. The case *Baum v. Boeing (China) Co.* was published by Judge Pallmeyer but written by the Boeing legal defense team and is filled with stunning inaccuracies and blatant deception.[5] and not even any mention or reference to the Chinese Court case where Boeing was found guilty. This injustice points to an egregious violation of my right to privacy, especially regarding my private medical information. This again highlights why the whistleblower system in America is absolutely broken, regardless if the complaint is against the government or corporations. I brought an Equal Employment Opportunity lawsuit against Boeing on grounds of discrimination and retaliation, and yet the outcome has proved severely damaging to my career and personal reputation. At West Point, cadets are taught to have the courage to speak up against unethical conduct. My doing so, however, has resulted in me missing out on being hired and even being terminated from my job on multiple occasions when my employer discovered this information about me on the internet. There is a real danger in speaking up against your unethical employer, and this dissuades would-be whistleblowers from coming forward.

Furthermore, the judge failed to properly inform me that my personal information would eventually be made public. After the verdict, I wrote the judge on three separate occasions, telling her how astonished and disappointed I am in her decision to not allow my case to go to trial and how I was never notified that my personal information would be made public. I informed the judge that the various internets sites told me if the judge sealed the contents of my case, then they would take down the information from the public websites. I have contacted Judge Pallmeyer on multiple occasions; however, she has denied my requests and allowed my private medical information to be published on the internet. She no longer responds to my communications, and her last communication with me is below:

Dear Mr. Baum:

There may be unusual circumstances in which a court ruling could be removed from the public record. In a case such as this one, where a ruling was placed on the court's docket months ago, I know of no realistic mechanism for cleansing the internet of any reference to it. More importantly, as I explained earlier, there is a presumption in favor of public disclosure of court rulings. I do not believe it is appropriate to depart from that presumption in this case.

Again, I am sorry I can't be of any further assistance to you.

Yours truly,

Rebecca R. Pallmeyer
Chief Judge

Judge Pallmeyer is once again wrong; my information regarding this court case can indeed be removed from the public internet, however it will as standard protocol, still remain in the internal government court database; she has the power to do us, however she has no ethical concern for justice. She thinks that making my private medical information available for public consumption is a good thing, as well as destroying my reputation and career by labeling me a sexual predator who was terminated from my job. By now, my privacy regarding this matter is a moot point, as I have already suffered significant damages to both my professional career and my personal well-being. Therefore, just like Judge Pallmeyer has already communicated her desire to allow the public to know all about my personal and sensitive information, let this be a warning to any would-be ethical whistleblowers of the retribution in store for you, should you wish to take a stand against the unethical government or corporations. If I had known this was how I was going to get treated by the American legal system, I would have saved my time and money and not have brought a whistleblower lawsuit against Boeing. This unethical judge has refused to even address the point of the Chinese court case. The same managers in Boeing who decided to terminate my employment are the very same Boeing managers against whom I filed discrimination claims; of course, they are going to have an unfair and unethical bias towards me. This is one of the reasons why I wanted to have the Chinese police involved. How Judge Pallmeyer does not understand this simple point and even fails to address it is pure unethical malice toward her actions to destroy both my character and career. Just by simply looking at the character of this judge, any American Patriot will realize that she holds the same unethical liberal, feminist, and communist ideology that is destroying America:

> Chief Judge Rebecca R. Pallmeyer announced today that she has appointed a Racial Justice Diversity Committee for the Northern District of Illinois. "Ongoing systemic racism has long existed in our nation, justice system, and legal profession. The Court recognizes that real change requires ongoing commitment and sustained effort. The appointment of a Diversity Committee is an important next step in examining and addressing these injustices. The Court is grateful to this

esteemed panel for undertaking this critical task for the Northern District of Illinois," said Chief Judge Pallmeyer.[6]

It's no wonder since she comes "down hard on the side of the 'equality feminists.' "[7]To Judge Pallmeyer, your actions regarding my case are a disgrace to the justice system of the United States of America. As an American citizen I was not only able to get my case with Boeing heard in the Chinese justice system, but I also received a resounding legal victory in China. In America, however, I was not even able to get my case heard, and I have thus suffered immense personal and career damages due to your negligence in publishing this information about me, without any prior warning or approval from me. Your actions demonstrate yet again how the rich and elite American corporations like Boeing buy their way to legal victory. I am an American veteran who honorably served my country, and you did not even grant me the chance to have my case heard before a jury of my peers. You preach all about the MeToo movement and that all victims have a right to be heard; however, in my case I am the victim of discrimination and yet you ruled that I do not even get the chance to have trial. Again, I am not even arguing about whether or not I would receive a legal victory in your court. I am simply arguing that I was not even given a chance to go to court. Your actions make a mockery of the American Legal System. You are in dereliction of duty by allowing my private medical information to be published on the internet without ever first notifying me about your intention to publish this information. After my repeated pleas, you have neglected to seal my sensitive information so it would be removed from the internet; this has resulted in numerous lost employment opportunities and even multiple job terminations. Never forget that your freedoms, your economic prosperity, your very government job and salary comes from the blood and sacrifice of American military veterans. Without service members' willingness to fight and die for America, your entire life and legal profession would not exist. The American justice system depends on American military men. How you a privileged federal judge who is funded on taxpayer money would deny a US citizen, let alone a military veteran, even the basic opportunity to present his case in court is an utter shame. After all the money I have personally spent, in addition to all the time and effort I poured into fighting for the chance to tell my story to a jury of my peers, your decision is not just an attack on my legal rights but an attack on all Americans who wish to right the wrongs done to them by these elitist globalist American corporations. Your unethical decision tells the American people that the American justice system is for sale. And furthermore, it showcases the hypocrisy of those who denounce the Chinese justice system as being unfair, corrupt, and unjust. I am living proof that the Chinese justice system, specifically in my case, is absolutely a more fair and just legal system than in America. Even as a foreigner, I was able to attain a victorious legal verdict.

Judge Pallmeyer, the next time you rant about your unethical and baseless fake feminist views, I want you to know that American women are actually the most privileged women in the world. No country in the world treats women better than Western countries like America. I am a 100% supporter of real feminism; however, you are the typical fake feminist and immoral person. My leadership task for you, should you accept it, is to go visit an American military cemetery, and as you view the various grave sites, learn about those who sacrificed for America. Ask yourself:

> Why aren't there more females represented in the graves of these US service members?

Why weren't women drafted along with men to fight and die in America's wars?

Why are young American men still required to register for the selective service, but women are not?

If it was not for all those military *men* who sacrificed for America, you would not have a luxurious and financially rewarding platform to complain about your false claims of oppression and sense of female entitlement. Fake feminism is evil, and it has corrupted the hearts and minds of American women like yourself. You are not qualified to legally judge in an unbiased and ethical manner. You censored my voice and denied my right to a trial based on your biased views. One thing that I respect about the Chinese society is that they have no tolerance for the fake feminism that is so rampant in America's crumbling liberal society. I recommend that you seek leadership counseling from your religious, philosophical, or spiritual advisor and request forgiveness. God will forgive; he forgives all who repent; however, repentance must be delivered and then therefore I will forgive you too, as God wills.

Do the harder right over the easier wrong even when no one is looking.

Remember that God is always watching, and you will ultimately be judged for all you do.

Amazon

After my illegal and unethical dismissal from Boeing, I moved to Hong Kong in attempt to find work. The situation in mainland China was changing. Nationalism and xenophobia were on the rise, and more and more western expats were leaving China. Rumors of war with America became more and more pronounced. It was while I was doing consulting work in Hong Kong that I landed my next job, with Amazon. Luckly during the Amazon hiring process my Boeing legal case was not yet posted on the internet, otherwise my application would have been rejected or rescinded which has now been a normal occurrence for me. Even though it is illegal for companies to retaliate against EEOC whistleblowers, companies do it all the time; and my career has suffered dramatically, with me being frequently unemployed due to companies refusing to hire me or even outright terminate me. There were two occasions where I was terminated from my job after my employer discovered this information. Both of these unethical employers (Kimberly Clark and GEODIS) illegally terminated my employment and yet they both continue to falsely proclaim how much they support military veterans and how much they are against discrimination.[8]

Therefore, with my EEOC lawsuit information having not been made public yet, I was able to pass through the hiring process with Amazon and was hired as the Head of Crisis Management for the Asia-Pacific (APAC) region. Amazon wanted to station me in Beijing, China; hence I would have to return to mainland China. Due to the growing nationalist tensions in China, I attempted to persuade Amazon to allow me to remain in Hong Kong or be allowed to be stationed in another APAC country instead. My job did not need to be stationed in China as evident by my predecessor, who was a foreign national stationed in Singapore. Amazon insisted that I be stationed in

Beijing; therefore, I reluctantly returned to mainland China. Within months after I began my work with Amazon in Beijing, the Covid pandemic erupted, and I was in full throttle crisis management mode in the APAC region. My performance was exceptional and as a result, Amazon management broadened my scope of responsibility beyond APAC to cover both India as well as the Middle East North Africa (MENA) regions. As the months turned into years, the Covid situation in China, as well as the rise of Chinese nationalism, produced a mass exodus of Western expats rushing to leave China. The brutal lockdowns in China were a nightmare, and my desire to leave reached a tipping point. In the previous years, I had made numerous formal requests to Amazon management in Seattle that I would pay for all my relocation costs and would be willing to relocate to any country in APAC; I just wanted to leave China for my safety. My requests were denied. In the spring of 2022, I just could not take the situation in China anymore due to a multitude of reasons including:

> Rising anti-American hatred
>
> Rising xenophobia against foreigners
>
> Rising racism against non-Asians
>
> Rising nationalism due to the threat of war with America over Taiwan
>
> Brutal Covid lockdowns
>
> Unwelcome solicitations in the Amazon Beijing office from fellow employees regarding my previous work with the US government
>
> Inability to openly and safely attend Jewish religious services

Senior Amazon management, none of whom has never lived in China nor even understand China, gave me no support. I even sent two formal petitions to Jeff Bezos (founder) and Andy Jassy (CEO) as well as to the other key Amazon executive managers, explaining to them how my job does not require me to be in China. I told them how I offered to pay all my relocation fees and would be willing to work in any APAC country besides China. I just wanted to leave China due to safety reasons. Despite my pleas, Amazon management simply told me that I either work in China or quit Amazon. Therefore, I decided to quit Amazon and leave China. Although I was faced with the stress of being unemployed yet again, my mental health immediately improved after I left China.

Reflecting upon this event, I have nothing against the country of China. Every country has the right for self-determination in how they wish to operate their domestic policy. No one invited me to China; I was a guest, a foreigner, and no one was stopping me from leaving China. Therefore, if I did not like the treatment I was receiving in China, then I was free to leave, which I did. I hold this same attitude for America and other Western countries. If you have ill feelings with your host country, rather than complain, insult, and demand it change its laws and culture to accommodate you, just leave. No one invited these immigrants or refugees to America. Should these foreigners not like the treatment they are receiving in America and other western countries, then they have the right and freedom to leave. The thought that America must accommodate the desires of foreigners is absolutely ridiculous.

Amazon, like almost all American corporations, preach the importance of diversity, equity, and inclusion (DEI), yet they only push their liberal ideology in Western countries. In China, Amazon's workforce was not even close to diverse, equitable, or inclusionary. There was absolutely no push to create a more diverse and multicultural environment in Amazon China. To add insult to injury is the fact that immediately upon my departure from Amazon, my job description was rewritten to allow my successor to be stationed in any country in the APAC region. And that is exactly what happened. Amazon hired a foreign national to replace me, and he chose to be stationed outside of China. In this very same role, both my predecessor and successor (both foreign nationals) were allowed to be stationed outside of China. The American veteran and former intelligence officer, however, was required to work in Beijing, China.

What is even more unethical and unpatriotic about Amazon is that, like Boeing, a significant portion of its revenues come directly from US government through government contracts. These government contracts are directly with the military-industrial complex. For example, Amazon Web Services continue to expand its reach inside the intel community with contracts like the $10 billon cloud computing contract with National Security Agency, a $600 million cloud computing contract with the CIA, and a $9 billion cloud computing contract with the Department of Defense. So again, the question needs to be asked: why are American corporations who are part of the US military-industrial complex allowed to do business with the Chinese government? This is an obvious conflict of interest to American citizens.

American corporations make money from US taxpayers as they lobby the US government to increase its security posture from threats like China. At the same time, these same US corporations are in China working with the Chinese government to make China stronger.

These American globalist corporations are traitors to the American people. They cannot be trusted. To Jeff Bezos and Andy Jassy, while both of you, gentlemen, were enjoying your luxurious and safe lifestyle in America, I was your employee in Amazon China, where I was not safe. Never forget, gentlemen, that a key factor to Amazon's success, along with all other American corporations, was the sacrifice made by US military veterans to ensure America was a safe and stable country in which you were able to build a successful business and enjoy a life of freedom. You two gentlemen have forgotten the sacrifices made by American military patriots as both of you were more concerned with making profits by whatever means necessary. While in America Amazon constantly preaches and enforces a liberal culture of diversity, equity, and inclusion; however, in Amazon China there is no DEI. Less than one percent of your workforce in China are foreigners of non-Asian ethnicity. There is absolutely no drive or incentive from Amazon management to make the workforce in China more diverse. The Amazon China workforce is becoming less diverse as more foreigners are leaving China. After repeatedly notifying management of how I was experiencing racism and an unsafe work environment in Amazon China, both of you ignored my emails. Your corporation cherishes the intimate partnership with the Chinese government; however, both of you have no concern for American veterans like me. Neither one of you gentlemen have ever served in the military, so I do not expect either of you to fully understand the concepts of patriotism, honor, and loyalty to America and to the American citizens. The globalist Amazon corporation needs to rectify its immoral and unpatriotic management behavior. Therefore, my leadership task for both of you, should you accept it, is to reevaluate Amazon's relationship with the American people. What is your oath of loyalty to America and to

American citizens; that is the primary question to ponder. Furthermore, I recommend both of you seek leadership counseling from your religious, philosophical, or spiritual advisor and request forgiveness and education. God will forgive. He forgives all who repent; however, repentance must be delivered. Therefore, I will forgive both of you too, as God wills.

Chinese corporations are nationalist.
American corporations are globalist.

12

Nationalism Is Unity: Diversity Is Not Our Strength

I wholeheartedly embrace the international community and globalism. This book is not an attack on globalization but to expose America's unpatriotic preference for globalism over nationalism. I believe America should embrace globalization but not at the expense of nationalism. This is when President Trump said, "America first!". I was astounded to see how many Americans found this mantra so offensive when it was just plain common sense. This same nationalist rhetoric is found in almost all non-Western countries around the world. For example Chinese president Xijinping (习近平)[1] would never have to publicly state China first because it is just a plain fact in China. Of course the Chinese government puts China first above all other countries on earth.

Nationalism means engaging and trading with the international community but putting your own county and citizens first.

Diversity Lie

Americans have been brainwashed into thinking that diversity is our strength. Diversity for liberal communists means diversity of race, religion, gender, nationality, and sexuality but not diversity of beliefs or ideologies. To even question this communist ideology is a sure fire way to get terminated from a corporate American job or ejected from an American university. Liberals refer to this diversity as essential for building a utopian rainbow society. This rainbow society must be filled with people across the spectrum of diversity. In reality, the result of this warped rainbow ideology will in fact lead to a dystopian anarchy. For those who may disagree with me and are contemplating whether this rainbow theory would hold truth, go visit a military cemetery anywhere in the world. Notice the lack of diversity which exists among the military veterans buried there. What one will find is that most of these grave sites are filled with veterans who are not very diverse. In America, for example, most of the military veterans buried in these cemeteries will be classified as American by nationality, European by race, heterosexual by sexual orientation, Christian by religion, and male by gender. When those people buried in American military cemeteries reflect the diversity of what these liberals epitomize as the ideal diverse society, then I will believe in the merits of having a rainbow nation. Until then I will put my faith in the type of diversity that has been on display by those soldiers willing to fight and die for America.

If diversity is such a strength, then why are American corporations and banks so fond of doing business in China? Why do they praise China for its economic achievements and development? China is anything but diverse. Only 0.02% of the Chinese population is made up of foreigners, and the majority of them are of Chinese ethnicity

(Chinese Americans, Chinese Canadians, Chinese Australians, etc). Furthermore, around 95% of Chinese nationals are of the Chinese Han (汉族)[2] race. China does not celebrate diversity; it celebrates unity, and its unity is its strength, which is a strategic advantage to China. Unlike America, the Chinese civilization has survived for thousands of years. Part of their success as a culture and a nation is the connection between what is Chinese and what is China. These two entities are intertwined and are irrefutable. In order to be China, it must be Chinese and vice versa. Even with respect to Chinese living overseas (华侨),[3] they will always identify as Chinese and will always have a connection with their motherland even if they were born and raised in another country. There is nothing strange about this. It is quite normal to identity with one's ancestral homeland and racial ethnicity. Americans, however, have lost their identity. Ask one hundred Americans "What is American?" and you will likely get one hundred different answers. Then ask "What is NOT American?" and you will probably get no answers, meaning *everything* is American.

Regarding leadership, if everything is something (American), then that something is undefined; therefore, it is essentially nothing—a la Chinese Daoist philosophy (道教).[4] For example, can I claim that I am Chinese? Since I am ethnically not Chinese, it would be almost impossible. However, for an American is there anything preventing anyone from claiming they are American? As long as they have American citizenship we would all agree that they are American. However, besides the citizenship, are there any other factors that could determine whether a person is an American or not? The answer is very sad and dangerous as there are no other factors in determining what is American or not. America has turned into a multicultural wasteland where anybody and everybody is welcome to partake in the crumbling dream. There are no restrictions, no limits, no standards. Pretty much everything goes, and almost anyone in the world can become an American citizen.

Other Western countries have abandoned their restrictions as well. For example, what is German, French, or British? Very similar to America, anyone and everyone can claim to be European now. European citizenships and American citizenships are available for everyone in this world, and once one obtains the citizenship, then that person is a full-fledged American or European. This open citizenship idea may sound appealing and lofty at first glance; however, the danger lies with the very fact that there are no restrictions, no standards, no objections. The result will be that the value of an American citizenship will eventually decline, and so too will America, as the entire country will become culturally diluted in globalist communism.

Racism Lie

America is inundated with a barrage of propaganda calling it a racist country. American citizens, particularly European Americans, are constantly harassed for being racist, hate-filled people. This cannot be further from the truth. After living in many countries around the world, I can confidently claim that Western countries are in fact the least racist countries on earth and that western men are the least racist men on earth. There are no countries in this world that treat women, minorities, and immigrants better than Western countries. This propensity for extreme tolerance, diversity, and multiculturalism is not something to be proud of either. It is actually very dangerous to the very survival of Western countries. Regarding racism, the most tolerant and heartwarming gesture a country can give a foreigner is citizenship to your own country. Granting citizenship to a foreign immigrant, giving these people all the same legal rights to make America their new home, is the highest honor. America and Western countries have the most liberal policies in the world for granting citizenships to foreigners, which dilutes that honor. In fact, in America, if a foreigner gives birth to her child in America, whether she entered America legally or illegally makes no difference; once that child is born on American soil, that child will automatically be granted American citizenship, no questions asked. That is probably one of the most liberal (and ludicrous) citizenship policies in the world. It reflects just exactly why America is the least racist country in the world.

Let us compare this citizenship policy to non-Western countries. I have lived in China for more than ten years. Not only did I *not* receive Chinese citizenship, I also did not even receive permanent residence. If I were Chinese (meaning Chinese American), however, then I would have been granted citizenship—although I would have to give up my American citizenship as China does not allow dual citizenship. The point being is that only people of Chinese ethnicity are permitted to obtain Chinese citizenship. It would not matter if I married a Chinese woman, had Chinese children, spoke Chinese, lived in China for fifty years, worked for a Chinese company, graduated from a Chinese university, or even was born in China. All of this does not matter: No Chinese ethnicity equals no Chinese citizenship. By doing so, China is protecting itself from foreign influence and control. The Chinese government wants to ensure that the citizens of China remain ethnically Chinese, and I absolutely find no fault in that.

Let us take a look at another country, Singapore, who claims to be a modern multiracial and multicultural society. Looking closely, however, is it really? When was the last time you have ever met a white,

Black, Hispanic, Arab, or Jewish person who was a Singaporean citizen? The answer is almost never. The reason being is that Singapore has racial quotas on who can obtain citizenship. These racial quotas remain relatively constant. Let's look at how many people from different ethnicity can become Singaporean citizens:

76% percent are Chinese
15% percent of are Malaysian
7.5% percent of are Indian
1.5% percent of are other[5]

These racial quotas are strictly based on ethnicity as opposed to nationality, meaning if a Chinese person was applying for Singaporean citizenship, it would not matter if this person were a Chinese from China or Chinese-American. They would be applying under the Chinese quota for citizenship. This is true for both Malay and Indian ethnicities. Therefore it does not matter if the applicants are Indian or Malaysian citizens or Indian-Americans or Malaysian-Americans. The Singaporean government is specifically categorizing the applicants by ethnic racial quotas. At the bottom, you can see 1.5% for other. This *other* category is for applicants whose racial identity is not Chinese, Malay, or Indian; therefore, only an extremely small number of Singaporean citizens are permitted from other ethnic races. Furthermore, at the top, you can see 76% for ethnic Chinese. It is therefore guaranteed by law to ensure that ethnic Chinese will always represent the majority population of Singaporean citizens, and thus the Chinese Singaporeans (within a Democracy) will always have the political power as their voting block will always dominate at the polls. So when Singapore boasts of their success as a multicultural country, in reality it is not a multicultural country by any means compared to

Western countries; it is ultimately a Chinese state with significant international characteristics.

I want to make it crystal clear: I am not signaling out China or Singapore in particular. Nor am I saying that either of these countries' polices are wrong or unethical. Actually, I find their policies to be correct and justified. The point is, if one were to look at almost all non-Western countries, one will find that gaining citizenship is either not allowed or almost impossible as an ethnically foreign applicant—especially if you are purely trying to obtain citizenship through naturalization as opposed to already having met one of the following helpful criteria, which may aid (but not guarantee) your citizenship application like being married to a local national or having been born in the country.

If you are just planning to move to a non-Western country and obtain citizenship purely through naturalization, then you will realize just how hard—and in most cases impossible—it is to obtain citizenship. More important, if you did indeed obtain citizenship as an ethnically foreign national, how much racism would you experience in the non-Western country. For example, if you decided to run for public political office, how would the locals view you? Would they welcome you to lead their country even though you are a Citizen of that country, even if you spoke the language and integrated into the culture? Any American who has spent time abroad in non-Western countries will realize that in no form or fashion would an ethnically foreign person be allowed to fully fit in. He or she would almost always be viewed and treated as a foreigner and as an outsider. In comparison, look at America. Not only are foreigners granted American citizenship through naturalization, many even go on to hold public office.

According to the Pew Research Center regarding the US government elective officials:

1. Immigrants and children of immigrants make up at least 14% of the 117th Congress.
2. There are eighteen foreign-born lawmakers in the 117th Congress, including seventeen in the House and just one in the Senate, a Hawaiin Democrat who was born in Japan.
3. Women make up just over a quarter of all members of the 117th Congress – the highest percentage in U.S. history and a considerable increase from where things stood even a decade ago.
4. About a quarter of voting members (23%) of the U.S. House of Representatives and Senate are racial or ethnic minorities, making the 117th Congress the most racially and ethnically diverse in history.

Compare these statistics above with any non-Western country, and you will instantly see that America is leading the way on diversity, inclusion, and multiculturalism. Yes, there is still racism and discrimination in America; however, what non-Western country on earth delivers better treatment and legal rights to these three groups. Again, one will find that America is actually the least racist country on earth, and Americans are in fact, the least racist people on earth. Perhaps the reason for the growing anger among the conservative patriots is because they are constantly labeled as racists when in reality they are the least racist people in the world.

If America was such a racist country; then why do so many people from around the world want to immigrate to America. The fact is, America is still a beacon of hope for many people from around the world who dream of immigrating to America and becoming American citizens. The problem rests on the principle of reciprocity. It is not fair to American citizens for immigrants to be allowed to enter America and subsequently obtain American citizenship. Should this situation be reserved, Americans would not be allowed to obtain citizenship from these immigrants' countries in the same manner. Briefly put:

If I cannot obtain citizenship in your country, then why should I allow you to obtain citizenship in my country?

Security and Safety

The goal of a government is to administer, improve, and maintain the security and economics of a country. It does not matter if the government and political system of a country is communism, fascism, socialism, or a democracy. All governments around the world and throughout history have had two main priorities to ensure the survival and prosperity of the country and its people:

1. **Economics**: The goal of every government is to constantly increase the effectiveness and efficiency of supplying the equivalent amount of goods and services to the citizens of a country that are in demand from these same citizens. All countries and all people throughout the world want to improve the state of their economic affairs. This is a universal desire to which all governments strive to meet.

2. **Security**: The goal of every government is to ensure its citizens are able to conduct their business and live their lives safely and feel protected in their personal lives. All countries and all people throughout the world want to feel safe. This is a universal desire to which all governments strive to meet.

The primary mission of all governments is security and economics, and the American government has been steadily failing in its mission. Through big government and big corporations both the security and economics of America continues to fail. In my case my government has failed to protect my security. Its treasonous and unconstitutional actions against me have undermined my economics and safety. Spying on American citizens, especially due to their political views, without legal due process is a threat to the constitutional protections and rights of citizens to feel secure and safe from unethical government overreach.

Two key industries or sectors where leadership is best showcased in security and economics are businesses and the military.

Businesses are the backbone of the American economy. Entrepreneurs and business leaders understand how to create, build, and preserve wealth. They are risk takers who gamble their own personal assets and resources in the hopes of attaining future financial rewards. They understand the stress, fears, obstacles, and unknowns that go into both managing and leading a business. They also understand the headaches and joys of being responsible for their employees, ensuring they have a stake in the dream and the company's success. They ultimately are leaders.

The Military is the security of a nation. Military service is the greatest sacrifice and loyalty one can give to the nation. Military leaders understand the dangers that threaten a country and its citizens. They are bold and battle hardened. They are warrior leaders who have answered the patriotic call of leading America's sons and daughters into battle. They are winners who understand there is no substitute for victory. If the war is lost, the nation will fall. They put the people and mission first. They are the knights of honor, sworn to fight and die for their land and people. They ultimately are leaders.

When it comes to security and economics, military and business leaders are the most trained, skilled, and accomplished members of society who can best deliver results to the citizens. Business leaders are the experts on the economy. Military leaders are the experts on how to improve and safeguard national security. Regarding American politicians, however, these two types of people are seriously lacking in representation in our Congress. According to the Pew Research Center, far fewer members of Congress now have direct military experience than in the past. In the 118th Congress, ninety-seven members served in the military at some point in their lives – a 58% drop since 1973, according to *Military Times*. There are more than twice as many Republican veterans (72) in the new Congress as Democrats (25). So, if business leaders and military leaders are not the primary candidates to serve Americans in government, what is the primary background of American Politicians? In total, more than half of all presidents, vice presidents and members of Congress in U.S. history had a background in law. Furthermore, more Democratic politicians are lawyers as compared with Republicans. So basically, the largest professional group of American political leaders are lawyers. Let us look at leadership and lawyers:

1. Lawyers in the Company: The highest position of leadership in a company is the CEO. Lawyers have a supporting role and not a leadership role. The head lawyer acts as the chief counsel. His or her job is to provide the CEO with legal advice or counsel. The job of the chief counsel is about supporting the company's mission and not about command. The chief counsel is not directly responsible for profitability; that responsibility goes to the CEO.

2. Lawyers in the Military: The highest level position of
    leadership in the military is the commanding general. Lawyers
    have a supporting role and not a leadership role. The head
    lawyer acts as the Judge Advocate General (JAG). His or her
    job is to provide the commanding general with legal advice or
    counsel. The job of the JAG is about supporting the military's
    mission and not about command. The JAG is not directly
    responsible for winning the war; that responsibility goes to
    the commanding general.

As you can see lawyers are not the leaders. Yet we have chosen
lawyers to be our leaders politically. What do these lawyers know about
security and economics? They have never served in the military, nor
have they ever run a business. The American people continue to elect
politicians who are not the ideal candidates to the primary mission of
America: security and economics. The American government needs
more business leaders and more military leaders as they both have the
two critical skills and backgrounds needed to guide America safely to
economic prosperity.

The same can be said for the senior leadership positions in
government, which deal with economics or security. For example, the
directors of both the FBI and CIA should be filled only by military
veterans. They know how to achieve mission success and how to
handle top secret intelligence, and understand the seriousness of
national security. It is time to get more business and military leaders
into our government instead of having a government that is flooded
to over capacity with bureaucratic lawyers.

The Chinese government's makeup, on the other hand, is filled
with the following demographics of Chinese citizens:

- Primarily all men
- Primarily all Han ethnicity

- Primarily all military or business backgrounds
- All born and raised in China

The American government needs more business and military leaders. We don't need more lawyers. America has too many lawyers as it is. This is one of the main reasons why America is collapsing. These lawyer-politicians do not grasp the essential elements of leadership with regard to security and economics.

Citizenship Riddle

Why isn't permanent residence enough?
Why do immigrants need US citizenship?

Why do immigrants/refugees need to be granted American citizenship in order to accomplish their goals in America? Or for that matter what is America's goal in allowing immigrants to enter the country. By granting immigrants with permanent residence as opposed to American citizenship, what exactly is not being accomplished? When these immigrants are eventually granted permanent residence, they will be able to legally live, work, and enjoy the American life. And more important, they will have the legal right to make America their permanent home. Why do immigrants *need* to be given the privilege of becoming American citizens? This need to grant citizenship is something happening only in Western countries. In non-Western countries, like Singapore, for example, many Westerners are permitted permanent residence (if they are lucky) but almost never become Singaporean citizens. Also, when comparing the benefits of permanent residence versus citizenship, one will realize that almost all the benefits are the same between these two classifications except the following:

1. Only American citizens have the right to vote.
2. Only American citizens have the right to work for the US government.
3. Only American citizens are afforded the full legal constitutional protections.

Who should *not* be granted American citizenship?
What is *not* considered American?
What is the difference between an American citizen and a citizen of a foreign country?

Use these questions above as the topic of discussion for your next intimate gathering of friends and family. To understand the leadership dimension of nationalism, one must ponder what citizenship is and how citizenship is at the heart of nationalism. For example, are there *any* exceptions to becoming an American Citizenship? Think about it. Ask yourself and your friends the following questions:

1. Regarding religion, can an American citizen belong to *any* religious group?
2. Regarding race, can an American citizen belong to *any* race?
3. Regarding political affiliation, can an American citizen belong to *any* party?
4. Regarding language, can an American citizen speak *any* language?

Is there *anything* that would preclude someone from not being considered an American citizen? Of course, having a terrorist background would certainly prevent someone from acquiring American citizenship. However, are there any other factors that would provoke someone to say yes, that person is American, or no, that person is not American? The leadership lesson here is:

If something is everything,
Then everything is nothing.

If US citizenship is open to everyone without restriction, then being American is equivalent to being *anything* and *everything*. This is of course a recipe for disaster. What if this same concept were applied to becoming a West Point Cadet. What if anyone and everyone was accepted into West Point regardless of the language they spoke, their fitness level, their competency or intelligence, or their ideology. What if there were no restrictions at all? Then the question would be: What exactly is a West Point Cadet? Everything means nothing, and that is exactly what West Point would become—and is currently becoming: Nothing.

The American people need to start having *safe* and *open* dialogs on this subject because America does not belong to the government or the corporations. America belongs to the people, and American citizens have a right and duty to decide who is allowed to become part of the extended American family. If Americans are unwilling or insecure with embracing, debating, and deciding on the concept of US citizenship, then leadership nationalism will never succeed. And America as a country will not survive.

I am willing to give my life to protect my
fellow Americans, the Soldier said.

Who are Americans? someone asked.

They are my people, so when I die in battle
they will not abandon me. They will ensure
my dead body is safely returned to America,
my home. They will visit my grave and
remember my sacrifice. They will never
forget me, because I have never forgotten
them.

13

European Replacement: Forbidden Topic of Discussion

One of the joys with living in China was the lack of racial tensions, which are omnipresent in America. The reason why China does not have any significant racial tensions (except in Xinjiang) is because China is not a racially diverse country. Only 0.02% of the Chinese population is made up of foreigners, and most of these foreigners are of Chinese ethnicity—Chinese Americans, Chinese Canadians, Chinese Australians. It is truly rare to see white, black, Indian, Arab, or Hispanic people in China. If you do, it will most likely only be in a major city like Shanghai or Beijing, and more specifically in the foreign expat community district in the city. China's level of diversity is not even close to America's or even Europe's. That lack of diversity allows Chinese citizens to live a life free from racial tensions that are ubiquitous in America. Yes, it is true there are actually fifty-six different ethnic minorities (少数民族)[1] in China; however, this does not cause any problems for two reasons:

1. The main ethnic group in China, the Han Chinese (汉族), makes up around 95% of the total Chinese population; therefore, the Han have a dominant presence in China.
2. The remaining 5% of the Chinese Population consists of fifty-six different ethnic minority groups which share such

similar Chinese DNA. Racial tensions are truly minimal to none.

For two years I lived in the city of Kunming (昆明)[2] located in the Chinese province of Yunnan (云 南). [3] Yunnan is the most Southwestern province in China; it borders Tibet to the northwest and Myanmar, Laos, and Vietnam to the south. Yunnan is the most ethnically diverse province in all of China, being home to twenty-six out the fifty-six Chinese ethnic minorities. Despite this I never witnessed any form of racism or segregation. All the people of Yunnan live in relative harmony. The reason being is that almost eveyone has similar genetic features. For the typical Westerner, it is extremely difficult to tell the difference between the Han Chinese and the Chinese of an ethnic minority. The one ethnic minority in China that does not resemble the Chinese people are the Uyghurs (维吾尔族) located in Xinjiang (新建). Urumqi (乌鲁木齐) [4] is the capital of Xinjiang. I have been there on three different occasions and have spoken with many of the local Uyghurs. As soon as I saw them, I knew there would be a major problem with their integration in China for three specific reasons:

1. **Race**. The Uyghurs do not look like Chinese. They are in fact of Turkic ancestry and ethnicity. They resemble Central Asians rather than East Asians. When I visited Xinjiang, I had already lived in China for over five years. I was truly shocked when I first saw the Uyghurs. They don't look Chinese!

2. **Religion**. China is home to three predominate religions: Taoism, Buddhism, and Confucianism. Western religions like Christianity and Judaism are unofficially recognized in China and are rarely practiced and then usually in secret. Islam, on the other hand, is prevalent among the certain Chinese ethnic minorities. Due to the numerous domestic terror attacks by

mostly Muslim Uyghurs, the Chinese government has cracked down on Chinese Muslims. Therefore, the Uyghurs strong devotion to Islam is not only at odds with the three predominant Chinese religions, it is seen as a significant threat to national security as well.

3. **Culture**. The first thing I noticed when I began speaking with the Uyghurs was that their Mandarin was bad. I was amazed at how much more fluent in Mandarin I was than almost all the Uyghurs. The Uyghurs prefer to communicate in their local dialect language. What shocked me even more was that the Uyghurs use their own written language too. Despite the many different dialects, throughout China everyone uses the simplified Chinese（简体字）5 as the common written language, however not the Uyghurs. Their written language is some type of Arabic script, which I did not understand.

In an extremely homogenous country like China where almost everyone looks, acts, and thinks the same, I immediately realized that there would be a major problem with the integration of the Uyghurs in China—and indeed it has been disastrous. The topic of race in China is so straightforward unlike in America or the West where the liberal Left continues to flip flop over their staunch racial theories.

First, the liberals preach that we are all the same; there are no differences in race. We are all human beings. Race is just a social construct.

**Race does not matter. We are all humans
with no differences.**

Then they tell us we need diversity. America is too white. Having different racial groups in American will be culturally enriching. We should cherish our diversity.

Race does matter. We are different and therefore we need diversity.

In China, a citizen's ethnic race is taken very seriously, to the point that their race is officially registered in the government database and even displayed on their national identification card (身份证).[6] That allows the officials to clearly see whether someone is Han or one of the fifty-six ethnic minorities. In China, race (along with gender) is definitely not a social construct. The Chinese take a lot of pride in their race and frequently compare the Chinese with other ethnic groups.

With regard to population decline, China, like most other non-Western countries, takes a radically different stance than America. In China, like in Japan, the population has already begun to decline, and China's answer is not immigration. Instead, the Chinese government is pulling out all the stops in incentivizing and supporting its citizens to have more children. The Chinese government makes it known to its people that they are essential to the survival and prosperity of China.

In contrast, the American government (both the Republicans and Democrats) constantly reminds its citizens that they are replaceable, that immigration is vital to the future survival and prosperity of America. Basically, the American government is telling its people that they *need* immigrants or America will not prosper. It is such an insult to the American citizens and a sharp contrast with non-Western countries like Japan, China, and South Korea.

American Government: Immigrants are essential to America. Therefore, Americans must welcome them with open arms. If you don't you are a racist. It does not matter if America's birthrate is low; the American government can replace its citizens with foreign immigrants. America belongs to everyone in this world.

Chinese Government: Immigrants are not essential. Furthermore, they do not belong in China. China belongs to the Chinese and we (the Chinese) will find a way to prosper without relying on immigrants.

Decline of the West

Americans cannot even talk about the continued decline of the white European population without being labeled a white supremacist. It is amazing to think that military veterans who fought to defend the freedoms of America are not allowed to voice their opinions without being called a conspiracy theorists or racists. Why is the replacement theory such a controversial topic? Americans can talk about the evils of China or Russia and how they are a danger to America, and they generally will not suffer any consequences. However, if anyone brings up the topic of white European replacement in America, they are immediately censored and condemned.

Permitted Topic: China and Russia are evil

Forbidden Topic: European replacement

Freedom of speech is vital in a democracy. A government and society that does not allow free and open speech is no longer democratic and free and should make the reader ponder. Why are military service members constantly being sent off to foreign countries to kill and destroy in the name of freedom if these very same American veterans cannot return home and enjoy the freedoms that they had just supposedly fought for? Freedom of speech is one of the most vital elements of a free society, and this freedom in America has been constantly eroded by big government and big corporations.

Whatever topic that you are *not* allowed to talk about is the manifestation of the true enemy.

This is why America's ridiculous and unconstitutional mission to stamp out hate by banning or censoring free speech will not work. Whatever problems exist in society, if the citizens are not allowed to openly talk about their problems due to fear of retribution, then they will seek secret forums to communicate with only other trusted members. Then US federal law enforcement will spend taxpayer money to penetrate these secretive groups and spy on American citizens. America's best effort to battle against so-called hate or extremism is to allow open and frank discussion.

China's unity is a strength.
America's diversity is a weakness.

Does anyone think that if the white European population in America continues to decline, there will not be any serious consequences. Is race really not that important? Is it truly just a social construct? And finally, if America's white European population drops to a minority, does one think that America will not be critically affected? Just look at South Africa where white Europeans make up around 10% of the population, yet there are alarm bells shouting about white genocide from the local white South Africans. They have been muffled by the international liberal media as racist conspiracy theories. During my time in China, I was surprised at the number of white South Africans I met and was curious as to why they immigrated to China. I was curious to know what was their backstory. The majority of them told me that

1. There is a white genocide going on in South Africa, and they were being displaced and marginalized. They didn't have a future there, so they left for a better and safer country. The discrimination against whites is unbearable in South Africa.
2. They preferred to immigrate to Western countries; however, Western countries refused to grant them refugee status. The visa restrictions and the financial burdens were too difficult; therefore, they moved to China, where at least it is a safe and developing country with work opportunities.

There is only one racial ethnic group in America with whom I truly sympathize: the Native Americans. It should be no secret by now; that this group of people was subjected to the horrific crime of genocide. Diversity and immigration were definitely not friends to the Native Americans. I am by no means saying that the Native Americans were a peaceful and innocent people. On the contrary, they were slave owners who were responsible for many savage and barbaric acts.

Nevertheless, genocide should never be condoned, and Americans must correct its historical error before it takes the moral high ground on similar issues. Before white European Americans can address the point about white genocide in America, we must first recognize Native American genocide and the suffering it has caused.

**Humans want unity with respect to our homes; however,
Humans want diversity with respect to our world.**

In America we must have the courage to talk about these racial topics regarding the safety and prosperity of all races. There will of course be disagreements and conflicts between races; that is what diversity will bring; however, there will also be many times where we can put our racial differences aside and work for the common good. However, we must all feel safe and secure; that our own race will live on and thrive. When I moved to China; I specifically wanted to see Chinese people, hear Chinese language, and experience Chinese culture; it was an absolutely culturally enriching experience; and I wish the Chinese people and the country of China a long and successful future. Years ago, I heard a story from a Chinese friend of mine who took his family from China to go visit Paris. His family took a vacation to Europe because they wanted to see European people, hear European languages, and experience European culture. When they arrived in Paris, they were absolutely terrified at how few white native Europeans are actually French citizens. To the family's shock, Paris had already turned into a liberal globalist multicultural mecca. The one most important thing that this Chinese family specifically traveled to France to see—French people—was lacking. Although the people in France are indeed French citizens, as my Chinese friend stated, "The majority of those people were not Europeans. Europeans are white people; everyone knows that." Due to fears over his family's safety, and their disappointment at not being able to experience an authentic European-style vacation, they abruptly ended their trip and returned to China. My Chinese friend was very disappointed. He was shocked at how many black people he saw in Paris. As he put it: "If I wanted to see black people, I would have gone to Africa. I specifically took my family to Europe because we wanted to see European (white) people."

When I lived in China, I was able to enjoy an authentic Chinese experience. When my Chinese friend visited Europe, on the other hand, he was not able to enjoy an authentic European experience. Why is it that China has been able to maintain and keep China, Chinese for thousands of years? If China can do it, why can't Europe maintain and keep Europe, European?

**The survival of one's people is
non-negotiable.**

Common Ground

There are elements to humanity that can help bridge the gap of racial diversity, like religion, for example. As a military veteran, I find common ground with fellow veterans regardless of their backgrounds. In one case, I am proud to call Eric Faqir, who happens to be African American, my friend. I met Eric during my first months as a brand-new field agent with the FBI. Eric is an accomplished martial artist and Yoga instructor, who operated his own yoga and martial arts studio. I was thirty years old at the time, and Eric was twenty years my senior; however, for a fifty-year-old he was impressive to say the least, not only mentally and physically fit, but also of good character.

When I first met Eric, he informed me that he was a veteran who had served in the US Army. We immediately struck a congenial chord; however, during my second visit to his studio, he had some extremely strange and shocking questions for me. Upon entering his studio Eric abruptly asked me: "Are you here to arrest me?"

"Of course not. Why would I arrest you?"

"You are a cop, aren't you? I thought you are here to arrest me and that you really don't want to learn martial arts."

I was still confused with what Eric was talking about. I replied, "First off, what makes you think that I am a cop?"

"Just by the way you look, walk, and talk; I can tell that you are a cop."

When Eric so easily assumed correctly that I was a police officer, I surmised that he probably had some prior encounters with law enforcement—possibly even having been arrested before. I replied: "Well, if I were a cop, why would I arrest you?"

He then started telling me of his long history of run-ins with the police, his extensive criminal record, that he was convicted on charges of terrorism, and that he was currently wanted by the police. I was shocked and immediately got defensive and fidgety. It was just Eric and me in the studio. I was standing there in fitness clothes and immediately regretted leaving my FBI service issued Glock 19 and handcuffs in my undercover vehicle. With an apprehensive tone, as though I were in "fight or flight" mode, I asked him, "What are you wanted for? Do you mean there is an arrest warrant for you?"

Eric was confused, saying he was not sure. He thought it had something to do with terrorism. His answers sounded strange, and for my safety, I abruptly said, "Don't worry about it Eric. I am not here to arrest you, but let's reschedule our class. I need to do some things first. I will call you to reschedule." Eric nodded his understanding, and we said goodbye.

Upon leaving his studio, I immediately drove to the field office, where I immediately ran a criminal check on Eric. Sure enough he had a criminal record; however, he had no outstanding arrest warrants. I will not go into his exact crimes for privacy reasons, but in my judgement, he had already dutifully served his prison time and paid his price to society. He was fully entitled to live as a free man in society. I printed out his background report and called to reschedule our appointment.

During my next visit to Eric's studio, with his criminal report in hand, I told him: "Well, you definitely have an interesting criminal record and have had your fair share of encounters with police; however, you are not a terrorist, Eric, and there are no arrest warrants for you. So you can relax. I am not here to arrest you, but you are pretty perceptive. I am a cop; I am with the FBI, but I am here just to learn martial artists with you—that is all. I have brought your criminal record with me. I think we should sit down and go over it together, so you can better understand it. We are both military veterans; you can trust me."

Eric and I then sat down in his studio and went over his criminal record. As I got to know Eric, I realized that he never received a formal high school education. Reading and writing were difficult for him. He told me about his upbringing, which was definitely a much harder childhood than I had experienced. He enlisted in the Army as a way to better his life and was proud to be called a veteran. After leaving the military, his life was a struggle. He had many setbacks, including numerous run-ins with the law.

After about a month into our relationship, we got to become really good friends. During that time, I witnessed him struggle financially. He asked me to lend him some money to help his fledging business as his debts were mounting. I gave him eight thousand dollars as a sign of our friendship. Also, during this time Eric was dating a local woman, and they were having some difficulties. He said his girlfriend broke up with him because she thought he was a wanted criminal. He told her I could vouch for him and wanted to know if I would tell her that he was not a wanted criminal. I was happy to oblige and arranged to meet the girlfriend and communicate to her about Eric's criminal record in an official capacity. When I met her, I introduced myself as Special Agent Baumblatt of the FBI, and I presented her with Eric's criminal record. I went over each of Eric's convictions and allowed her to judge for herself the seriousness of each crime; however, I specifically stated that Eric was not a wanted criminal nor was he a terrorist. I told her Eric was a man of good character and that I considered him my friend. It was about a fifteen-minute meeting, and I left thinking that would be the end of this matter.

As months went on, Eric's relationship with his girlfriend turned from bad to worse. She got a restraining order against him. When he didn't comply, he was sent to jail yet again. I would visit him in jail, several times, and he always maintained his innocence, saying his ex-girlfriend was lying. Eventually the restraining order violations, coupled with Eric's criminal background, brought him before a federal judge. Eric asked if I would be a character witness for him, and I agreed. A couple days later, I unexpectedly received a phone call from an Assistant US Attorney, the federal prosecutor, who would be prosecuting the case against Eric. This prosecutor was amazed that an FBI agent would testify as a character witness for Eric. On the call, she even threatened me by saying that if I testify in defense for Eric, it would ruin my FBI career. She began interrogating me on the telephone. She wanted to know all the details regarding our relationship. She told me that an FBI agent should not be friends with a criminal like Eric. She then became "unhinged" when during my conservation with her she found out that I lent Eric eight thousand dollars. Having never received the money back, the prosecutor became very suspicious of my relationship with Eric. When I told her our relationship revolved around martial arts and yoga, she laughed. She implied that Eric and I were collaborating in some type of illegal activity together. "So, David, are you trying to tell me that you just met Eric and within a couple of months he is already your good friend to the point of giving him eight thousand dollars of your own money on a government salary? This does not seem normal. Are you and Eric involved in any criminal activities together?" she asked. "Your relationship does not make sense; and you are in trouble of jeopardizing much more than your FBI career."

I could tell she was a typical fake feminist, as well as a typical leaderless lawyer who was hellbent on not only putting Eric back in prison but also anyone else in her way. At that point, her unprofessional and immoral conduct had reached its limits with me. I asked her if she had ever served in the military. No, she replied. I told her that during her entire deprecating rant characterizing Eric as a thug she never once pointed out that he is a military veteran. I told her that

Eric had volunteered to defend our country and honorably served in the US military. He is entitled to that respect; he earned it. I carried on by saying, "Since you have never served in the military, you do not understand the honor that goes along with it; both Eric and I are military veterans. We share that common bond, and that military bond is the foundation of our relationship." I could tell that she did not understand the concept of loyalty or brotherhood; however, I don't think most liberal globalists and fake feminists have ever understood it.

A couple weeks following my phone call with the federal prosecutor, my FBI supervisor called me into his office and told me that the FBI Office of Professional Responsibility (OPR) had initiated an internal investigation against me for allegations of misconduct regarding my relationship with Eric. All of the allegations against me were eventually found unsubstantiated and subsequently dropped, except for one in particular. During the final phase of the OPR investigation, I was called into the office to meet with two FBI managers who would be coordinating with FBI HQ as to decide on my ultimate punishment. Both managers acted very professionally and gave me the opportunity to tell my side of the story. The one element of the OPR investigation that remained was to examine my conduct regarding Eric's ex-girlfriend and possibly using my FBI status to influence her opinion of Eric. I used this OPR incident as a leadership lesson—and an opportunity to exercise courage and morality by admitting my faults. I fully admitted to the two FBI managers that I made some mistakes, which included talking to Eric's girlfriend in my official FBI capacity in order to unintentionally influence her judgement regarding Eric. Looking back, Eric's relationship with his girlfriend was a private affair, and I should have just stayed out of it. I admitted my fault regarding this action, and both FBI managers acknowledged my cooperation and thanked me for my candor to admitting guilt. In the aftermath, I received a two-week suspension of unpaid leave—not that harsh of a punishment; however, considering that I had been in the FBI for only a year and already had received an OPR violation, it was yet another bad omen.

I purposely revealed Eric Faqir's full name in the hopes of indirectly helping his cause. I have not had any contact with him for over fifteen years, and I do not know his current whereabouts; however, if my intuition serves me correctly, he probably is still in need of some friendly support. With his exceptional talent and good nature, any potential client will be very satisfied with the value that Eric will add to your life. His website seems to still be active: https://baguayinstyle.com/about-me. I recommend to anyone in the San Francisco area, if you are looking for a martial arts, yoga, or fitness instructor, then Eric is a great choice.

Never forgot that America is filled with people like Eric. There are many military veterans who have fallen on hard times and had less than optimal childhoods, and even though their conduct has sometimes proved to be wrong, they are willing to correct their mistakes and own up to their misdeeds. Military veterans have the ability to easily transcend racially ethnic bias. A true soldier is just that, a soldier—plain and simple, regardless of race, they are brothers in arms. The federal prosecutor involved in my OPR did not understand this concept, but hopefully the American public can. Thank you, Eric, for your service to the country and also for our friendship. You have walked a rocky road in your life, may you one day find peace with God.

Who finds a faithful friend, finds a treasure.
—Jewish Proverb

14

Faith: Leadership is Ultimately about Salvation

The study of leadership must encompass faith. Man's strength and courage are derived from his faith—whether that be from religion, philosophy, or spirituality. I follow the religious practice of Judaism. In addition, since childhood I have been studying and following the spiritual and philosophical teachings of Chinese Daoism （道教）. Within the religious framework of America, we must never forget, or allow ourselves to be convinced otherwise, that the history of America is one steeped in Judeo-Christianity. To embrace the roots and traditions of America, a country with European roots, one needs to recognize the significance and beliefs that Judeo-Christianity has had on the creation of America and the American people. The path of leadership rests on the path with God. We are all mortal men who ultimately seek the divination to the origin of time and space. Our wellspring rests in the hands of our creator. Without God, we are lost in the infinity of the Dao.

**May we die with honor,
and may God forgive us.**

When I entered West Point, like all incoming cadets, we were called plebes, and our first task was to successfully complete the Cadet Summer Basic Training, otherwise known as Beast Barracks. Having already graduated from Marion Military Institute and completed the Army ROTC program, earning a commission as a second lieutenant in the U.S. Army, I was well prepared for Beast Barracks. I was significantly more advanced on my leadership journey than most of my classmates, at one time I attained the second highest ranking in my class in the military leadership performance category. Cadets are ranked on their performance in three separate categories: academic, physical, and leadership. I always excelled at leadership; however, like all leadership evolutions in life, there will always be more chances to succeed and fail, as well as to learn and grow. This is how we develop as people.

West Point is a unique and historical leadership laboratory that is unlike any other. The athletic mascot of West Point is the Black Knight. Our black athletic uniforms set against the castle-like backdrop of the US Military Academy's formidable stone buildings gives the image of gallant knights training for combat in service to king and country. This image of the gallant knight became more clear to me during every passing day of Beast Barracks. At every morning roll call each cadet company, full of plebes, would stand in formation and sound off in unison with their respective company's battle cry. In the process they showcased their fighting spirit and motivation with the loudest and fiercest military command voices they could muster.

The Gladiators

Golf Company's mascot was the Gladiator, and they had an inspiring battle cry that always stood out to me. As each company (Alpha, Bravo, Charlie, etc.) took turns reporting to the higher cadet command, and thus shouting their respective company's battle cry, it soon got to Golf Company. I always took mental note in anticipation to their thunderous call to arms. Standing at attention and being a plebe, I dared not turn my head and look in the direction of Golf Company. I just stared straight ahead and intently waited to hear the Gladiators sound off. It always was done in the same manner: the upper-class cadet (the company commander) would stand in front of Golf Company and initiate the command by shouting in a thunderous voice:

GLADIATORS!!!!!!!!

The entire company would roar back:

WE SLAY THE BEAST!!!!!!!!.

The Gladiators of Golf Company were determined to slay Beast Barracks. Me and my fellow classmates would indeed go on to slay the beast that hot summer in the mountains of upstate New York just as a gallant knight would slay a dragon. There is something magical about West Point and the Black Knights. Through America's darkest days and longest nights West Point graduates have answered the call to arms. It is a legacy that can be traced back to the founding of America during the revolutionary war when General George Washington coined West Point the Key to the Continent recognizing its importance in preventing the British Navy from establishing superiority along the Hudson River. This magical legacy of the US Military Academy exists in the spirit of the Black Knights from West Point—as well as the beasts and dragons who wish to destroy America. Only during war and combat, when the dragon or beast is slayed, can the Black Knight raise his sword in victory, having only then the privilege of bestowing the honor yet again upon West Point, upon America, and most important, upon the American people.

In a dark world filled with less-than-honorable foes and even evil monsters, finding a Black Knight to champion the holy cause of God, King, and Country has become a journey longer and harder than most men can bear. However, there are still these Black Knights to be found in America. They reside in the shadows of the hopes and dreams of the pious American patriots. As America continues to stumble down the inevitable decline into the immoral abyss, these brave men will be summoned once again to lead the charge in bringing back what has been taken from America: **Faith, Family, Freedom**. One day, the Black Knights will return, much like our American forefathers, the Sons of Liberty, and they too will do battle with the forces of evil. For it is only in danger when a hero can emerge.

Become your own gallant knight and slay your own beast or dragon.

The American ethos of freedom has been forged through the centuries by the blood, sweat, tears of brave patriotic men. Despite the liberal propaganda claiming that America was founded by immigrants, on the contrary, our European forefathers never immigrated to

America. They left the safety and comfort of Western Europe in search for freedom, adventure, and opportunity. These brave men settled America; they did not immigrate to America. They were willing to risk their lives in negotiating the hazards of the voyage, the frontier, and the survival in a new uncharted and uncivilized land. They were willing to pay the ultimate sacrifice for the priceless reward of freedom.

Yes, it is true, that our European forefathers killed countless Native Americans in the process, that genocide is indeed part of our American history, and that we Americans should be willing to confess and be accountable to this fact; however, the result was nevertheless the establishment of the most exemplary country this world has ever seen: the United States of America. Despite the propaganda claiming America is a racist country, a continuous flow of countless immigrants from all ethnicities immigrate to America and become US citizens squashes that notion. The greatest strength of America is not our diversity but the freedom that America offers. That is the primary reason why immigrants want to come to America. Freedom is the primary reason why America is so great, and as this moral ideal of individual freedom declines, so too will the country of the United States.

Remember When

My father's favorite movie was *Jeremiah Johnson,* staring Robert Redford. My father would often say that he was born in the wrong time period. He wished he could have been a mountain man like Jeremiah Johnson, living off the land in the 1800s when America was wild and free. When a man did not depend on the government for help, but a man would depend on his own self-reliance for survival.

When the government was not yet powerful enough to control the lives of the citizens, and thus would leave the citizens alone to live their lives as they wanted—in freedom. When men's lives were connected more closely with the earth, and therefore they learned to respect the unforgiving power and cruelty of nature—they also wondered in the splendor of God's green earth. When hard work was accompanied by muscular effort and sweaty brows as opposed to modern-day men sitting all day in front of computers. When men needed to be strong, tough, and resourceful in order to provide and protect for their families. When women needed to be caring, loyal, and devoted to the children and to the leader of the family. When "organic food" was the normal food staple directly from the farm or from the wilderness, free from chemicals and genetically modified organisms. When America's territory was vast and open, as opposed to today's congested and crowded urban environments. When having a rifle and being able to use it for hunting and protection was the norm. When men were expected to be courageous in the fight and women were expected to be nurturing in the home. When people identified as proud Americans, as opposed to the constant racial subterfuge of today's liberal ideology. When men and women actually became parents and created close-knit families, as opposed to the lonely childless meaningless lives of today's depressed Americans. When working outside in the sunlight and living a healthy lifestyle in accordance with nature was the best form of medicine, as opposed to today's pharmaceutical industry's pill-popping lifestyle. When a woman's virginity was seen as noble and sacred, as opposed to today's promiscuous women who revel in their freedom to become dirty whores and OnlyFans prostitutes. When going to the church or synagogue and having an intimate relationship with God was paramount, as opposed to today's atheist culture where God is now a liberal progressive and who has suddenly changed his moral outlook on mankind. When a man's word was his bond and his firm handshake sealed the deal, as opposed to the legions of today's unethical lawyers who circle around like vultures searching for opportunities to propagate litigious discord.

America's morals have indeed changed over time, and therefore American society has also changed with it. Today's liberal progressive morality embraces a globalist love of the world where a communist utopia is envisioned and the dream that no one will own anything and like it. Except of course for the global elites who will indeed own everything, including your freedom, and who will indeed be even happier than you. In the elite's world you will eat bugs and drink soy milk while you live in your urban container dwelling free from any distractions like children and animals. Your identity will be completely null and void as you and the rest of your fellow plebes enjoy an atheist lifestyle devoid of God and full of digitally mindless entertainment. You will feel comfortable and safe because the government will have taken away all risks associated with the real world, and as long as you follow the rules and allow the government to control your life, you will never have to fear the risks that freedom brings. You will let go of the evils of individualism and embrace the righteousness of collectivism. As your leaders enjoy the privileges of power, you will enjoy the privileges of servitude. Your privacy will no longer be important because you will have nothing to hide. The government will have access to all of your information, but you will not have any access to the government's information nor of your political leaders. Everyone will be treated with respect as only respectful language will be tolerated. You will learn what to say and how to behave. The government will teach you how to become a good citizen, and a good citizen you must become; otherwise, your access into the digitalized society will be denied, and you as a citizen will be deleted. This is today's modern American culture. This is the path in which we are headed.

I wonder at all the active duty military personnel who are proud to be deployed overseas, fighting in the never-ending foreign campaigns. What exactly are these military service members fighting for? Our military is supposed to fight and defend the freedoms of US citizens. Do they share in this globalist communist utopia dream as well? What freedoms are our military personnel exactly fighting for?

Morality is what your heart and God tell you is right. Legality is what your head and government tell you is right.

The Devil guides the Godless

A godless man is lost in a world that no longer honors loyalty. Without loyalty there can be no leadership. American globalist corporations look upon their workers as widgets, and the workers look upon these corporations as machines. The globalist American government looks upon its citizens as taxpayers who serve at the behest of the state, and the citizens look upon the American government as a master elite.

As man becomes godless so too does society and then finally the entire country will find itself lost. Like a spy trapped in the wilderness of mirrors in which he has spent and consumed all of his betrayal until at the very end, he has finally deceived everyone until at last, he realizes he is the one who was deceived. He sits alone with a broken crown and a false flag. The godless globalist America is the land of corporate capitalism where everything has a price and freedom is indeed priceless. Godless America is where our government spies on its innocent citizens because it does not trust them. In return the citizens do not trust the all-powerful government. It is where the American military war machine rumbles on to invade yet another overseas target of economic opportunity, where the citizens of the empire that fights in the name of freedom and democracy are not even free to speak their own mind as the very basic freedom of speech is slowly being stripped away. As America becomes less American, the patriotic citizens become strangers in a strange land—no more community, no more home, both God and family are already dead. America has become a culture of increasing profits for the corporations as its citizens are supplied with the materialistic dopamine in an effort to numb them of the realities of their consumeristic lifestyles. Another beer, another ball game, another temporary high as the citizen widgets continue in their servitude to the godless globalist American empire. One day death will come, and it will all be over. How long can America last down this godless path? Sooner or later the widgets will no longer be able to grind along in the corporate machines. Sooner or later either the widgets break or the machines break. A breakdown is coming, and with it will come the rage against the machine. So help us God.

American globalist corporations have seduced man to become addicted to irrelevant matters of the consumer society. How pathetic the modern American man has become as he has allowed his life to revolve around following his favorite sports team, or the American woman around following her favorite fashion trends, or the American children around following their favorite television shows.

America has put actors, athletes, and celebrities on a pedestal. They worship these figures who provide nothing but mindless entertainment. As Americans continue to worship the false gods of corporate capitalism, they fall deeper and deeper into a lonely hole of depression. As the American government continues to clammer over its false "war on drugs," the American corporations continue to push drugs on the people. Intoxicated Americans have lost their way because without God they have no direction. Reaching for drugs will not solve the problem; however, reaching for the God will.

The American corporations despise God because God cannot be marketed or sold. Faith is free to all who wish to detach themselves from the American consumer world and believe in the everlasting journey of the soul. The globalist American government despises God because a faith-based citizenry fears no repressive regime.

In the times of milk and honey talks about God and faith seem unimportant and whimsical to the self-indulgent citizens, who are sedated on abundant amounts of bread and circus. However, when destruction and despair return with a vengeance, the weak-minded citizens are struck with terror that only the hand of God can shield them. God shall return. Actually, he has never left; however, he has become invisible in the eyes of the decadent liberal American society.

America has gone blind, and this madness is destroying the patriotic American ethos. Warrior leadership is coming, because, if not, then America will fall forever. The choice will be made by the American patriots who are the only warriors left to battle the communist beast that is growing in America.

Loyalty is Love

The single most destructive force in the moral decay that is destroying America is the abandonment to the leadership principal loyalty. Loyalty is the cornerstone of leadership; and without it; the people will not follow. Even the FBI's motto, Fidelity, has long been abandoned as the FBI management does not even trust their own agents (as witnessed by their immoral spy campaign against me); nor does it trust American citizens. This disloyalty is seen throughout the American government and corporations. Both the government and corporations are not loyal to the people; therefore, why should the citizens be loyal to the government and corporations. The American government continues to put foreign countries and foreign citizens above the welfare of the American public. It willfully spends American tax dollars on foreign endeavors that do not help American citizens.

In China, the government puts the country and its citizens above foreign countries and foreign citizens; China embraces nationalism. In America both our government and corporations put foreign countries and foreign citizens above America and American citizens when money dictates. They embrace globalism. This disloyalty has expanded to everywhere in American society to the point where American citizens have lost trust in the government, corporations, media, universities, religion, and even the military. The military was once a bastion of patriotism and loyalty, an organization that exhibited the highest degree of loyalty, trust, and valor and American military officers were looked upon as the most honorable, courageous, and patriotic people in society. I have since lost trust in American military officers—especially the career generals and admirals who have squandered their honor on their egotistical careers and their cowardly failure to stand up for the truth.

The FBI's spy campaign against me revealed just how disloyal some of my close associates were in their willingness to betray me. Some of these traitors are fellow West Pointers who I had previously sacrificed for and had personally helped throughout my life. I will not reveal their names, but they know who they are. I hope the money they received from the FBI was worth their betrayal of a fellow West Pointer. This is a nefarious omen cast upon the American people. When West Point graduates can no longer trust each other, then the splintering of the military has already begun—and civil war is around the corner. The FBI will hold no guilt in their promulgating moral deceit between fellow military veterans as their lack of leadership is synonymous with their lack of moral consciousness.

Probably the most powerful intelligence agency to ever exist was the Stasi of East Germany. Their ruthlessness and aggressiveness in collecting intelligence cloaked the East German people in darkness. The Stasi wanted to know every private detail regarding the lives of the East Germans, and they achieved success by convincing and coercing its citizens to betray each other. Whether it was a son spying on his own mother, a brother spying on his brother, or even a wife spying on her husband, the Stasi wanted everything. The East Germans lived in such a fear that they abandoned their morality and sense of loyalty in favor to their subservience to the communist state. In communist East Germany both God and the family were dead. The government replaced both and used fear to instill absolute loyalty to the state. In East Germany the citizens were paralyzed with fear of the surveillance state. East Germany collapsed due to the moral decline; the country turned into a prison. Privacy was replaced with surveillance, and loyalty was replaced with servitude. America is already heading down this same path.

Loyalty is the fire of leadership.
Brotherhood is forged in this fire.

The FBI's investigation into the violent January 6 protest is an immoral embarrassment to the FBI. To use the blanket term of domestic terrorism to describe the event and to label the protestors as domestic terrorists is a farce. During my time in the FBI we deemed Islamic extremists as terrorists. Now the FBI is labeling middle class and middle-aged American conservative men and women as terrorists. The FBI's investigation into January 6 protest has led to the arrest of many non-violent, tax-paying, patriotic conservatives. Their investigation persuaded so many Americans to betray their fellow friends and family members. As Americans turned on each other in their dubious service to the FBI, more and more arrests were able to be made through the disloyalty of friendship and family. The FBI's immoral actions would make the East German Stasi very proud. Having American family and friends renounce their loyalty to one another and then pledge their allegiance to the FBI is a great feat for any intelligence agency. The FBI's division and consequently destruction of family and friendships showcased just how immorally disjointed America truly is. If the government and corporations can break the loyal bonds of the American family, then they can control everything. It is time for Americans to embrace God. He is their only hope in the face of government tyranny.

To those West Pointers who have compromised their integrity by spying on me through the collusion with the FBI, you have not only tarnished your honor and family name but also the honor of the US Military Academy. If you are willing to deceive a fellow West Pointer, then you are willing to deceive fellow American citizens. As the honor of West Point graduates like yourselves declines, so too will the reputation of West Point—and then of America. The US military has lost the ethical mantel of leadership. As soon as the military is no longer loyal to the citizens, the people lose trust in the military. This is the last stage before collapse and civil war.

Where there is courage, there is no loneliness.
Where there is loyalty, there is love.

In America, loyalty has become a cliché. In a society where people are scrambling to get their next hit of dopamine from the newest and most influential source, citizens continue to self-indulge with their intoxicating addictions in a hyper digitally consumer-driven America. The concept of being loyal to someone through good times and bad is old-fashioned. Loyalty to your spouse, to your parents, to your employer, to your neighbor, to your friends, to your fellow citizens, and even to your own country are all outdated. Unless others can be of benefit to you, then you have no need for them. Once their usefulness has expired, then so too does the relationship. "Who is my brother's keeper?" asked the knight without armor in a war-torn land.

Even in politics there is certainly no loyalty—even from the voters themselves, as was displayed within the Republican Party. Ron DeSantis, Mike Pence and other Republican presidential candidates have entered the fray against Donald Trump. The leadership principle of loyalty should be applied here. I have nothing but positive remarks for Ron DeSantis; however, it was Trump, not DeSantis, who led the Republic Party into a new movement. The Make America Great Again (MAGA) movement, which is simply American nationalism, was a unique direction in which Trump took the Republican Party. Should any Republican candidate or voter for that matter; align themselves with this nationalist movement, then they should be loyal to the person who inspired and courageously created the movement. If Trump wants to pass the torch of leadership to DeSantis or another candidate, then that is his prerogative.

As societies and cultures experience declines in loyalty, it is a harbinger of eventual collapse. The bedrock of society rests with the family, and what is family without loyalty. Loyalty is the moral glue that holds relationships and bonds together as both parties are committed to one another based on certain inalienable principles through the covenant of man's relationship with God. For example, I have had my own family loyalty questioned by some of my Jewish friends when the discussion of World War II comes up, and my German grandfather's (*großvater*) honor is contested. I consider my German *großvater* (Hans Grube) to be an honorable man and someone who patriotically served in the German Wehrmacht, in defense of his country, his *Vaterland*, during World War II. As the grandson, I will always have the duty to honor and respect my family, including my German *großvater*. I have no doubt; that if my Jewish American grandfather (serving in the US military during WWII) and my German grandfather (serving in the German military during WWII) were both able to meet one another, they would find common ground and friendship. They would see each other as patriotic citizen soldiers who both had **duty, honor, country** as their guiding principles in life. They would also both see themselves as children of God who were forced to grapple with the struggles of life and loyalty, and to the best of their abilities strive to make the world a better place for their family, *volk*, and country.

Loyalty is paramount in leadership; and the United States government is failing in this regard. A case in point is how the US government seeks to become self-reliant and independent regarding its resources supplied from foreign countries. This is both a noble endeavor as well as keen to national security. I embrace international trade and cooperation, as well as overall globalism; however, I am a nationalist at heart. It is prudent for all governments and countries to become as self-reliant as possible. You can witness this with the US government's goal to become energy independent, food independent, and an increasing push towards supply chain independent (bringing factories back to America). What is the most important resource of a country, and also what is central to the idea of leadership, however, is its people. Without the people, there is no country. When it comes to people, though, the US government (and US corporations) fully support importing foreign immigrants. Regarding America's "dependence" on foreign immigrants, this is a different political matter. Globalist government and corporations call it a "good thing." According to them, it is good that America is **dependent on immigrants.** Why is it bad that America is dependent on foreign oil, foreign security, foreign commodities, but good that America is dependent on immigrants. The US government should help its citizens make families and therefore remove the dependency on immigration.

Many countries are experiencing population declines. China and Japan, for example, have decided that the solution to a dwindling population is to increase the birthrate of its native citizens, as opposed to opening the doors for immigration. The Chinese government has decided that the best people to replace the Chinese are with Chinese people. What if the Western governments had the same viewpoint: the best people to replace the Germans are with German people. The best people to replace the French are with French people. The best people to replace the Americans are with American people, and so on. Just like the US government does not want to depend on foreign countries to provide for its security, food, oil, energy, and commodities, it shouldn't want to depend on foreign countries to provide its people. The US government continually touts that dependence on foreign resources is a national Security issue. The most important resource of a country is its citizens. Therefore, why then is America's constant dependence on immigrants viewed as a strength?

A leader relies on morality.
A manager relies on legality.

15

Take Charge: Lead, Follow, or Get out of the Way

The Boy Scout motto, Be Prepared, typifies the mental attitude that all American patriots should be embracing as collapse and civil war are on the American Horizon. Although every patriot should be exercising their right to vote in the political elections, I unfortunately do not have faith in the American politicians' desire nor ability to remedy the catastrophic future that will befall America. Donald Trump is without a doubt the best option to attempt to sail the sinking ship of American decline. Even with him as president; however, I do not believe America will survive. Only American Politicians who honor these two ideals should be supported:

1. **Freedom**: Power must be returned to the people. As the government and corporations exert controls over the lives of American citizens, it deprives them of life, liberty, and pursuit of happiness. Patriotic American citizens are tired of having to give their tax money to the US government and then seeing it spent on programs that do not add value to their lives. The US government's tyrannical powers continue to increase and thus deprive Americans of their liberties, which was plainly evident during the Covid pandemic. I was living in China at the time and experienced the Chinese government's brutal lockdowns, which made me appreciate just how

precious individual rights and freedoms are. Freedom must be once again cherished and honored, and only those American politicians who vow to increase and defend the civil liberties of American citizens should be supported.

Spying on American Citizens via the FBI's unconstitutional use of FISA warrants should be abolished. American citizens should only support politicians who pledge to protect the freedoms of US citizens, whether it is in their homes, schools, businesses, organizations, or communities. All private entities within America should be returned to the powers and discretion of the American citizens where they should have complete freedom of association in deciding who will be accepted into their private lives.

2. **Patriotism**: American politicians can embrace globalism and international cooperation; however, they must always put America and American citizens first. American citizens should only support politicians who are nationalists at heart. It is time for Americans to only vote for America first political candidates. From liberal immigration policies to exorbitant foreign aid packages, the US government must be accountable towards the patriotic service to American citizens and make them their number one priority. Only true American companies should be entitled to receive the support of the American taxpayer. All other globalist corporations should lose any special taxpayer entitlements and government contracts.

The military-industrial complex must be thwarted with new rules restricting retired generals from seeking private employment within American defense corporations. All US politicians who rally for the support of these insidious and never-ending overseas military campaigns must be personally examined and judged. Are they military veterans who personally understand the consequences of war? or perhaps they have children who are serving or have served in the Armed forces? These questions must be asked. Far too often these chicken hawk warmongering politicians and their children, who have never had the courage nor the patriotism to serve in the US Armed Forces, have no problem sending other Americans serving to their death, fighting in these immoral overseas conflicts while at the same time continuing to increase the debt of the US taxpayer. Border security must be achieved, and the immigration system needs a complete overhaul. Birthright citizenship must be abolished and granting permanent residence as opposed to granting US citizenship must be the preferred norm for qualified immigrants. We live in a global world. International cooperation is not only good, it is a necessity; however, only those politicians who adamantly proclaim and are also proud to be labeled as nationalists should be supported.

To those US politicians who disagree with my assertion that big globalist government is the enemy of the American people, I challenge you to restore individual freedoms to the American people and also restore patriotism to America. If you are a patriot, then I welcome your efforts and duty to leading America through the disaster that will eventually befall it.

I challenge the corporate CEOs to put America first with regard to the hiring and promotions within. I also challenge you to bring back jobs and production to America. I finally challenge you to exercise deep thought in ensuring your products or services are in the best interests of America and Americans. If Americans are expected to buy American products, then American corporations are expected to prioritize hiring American citizens.

In the name of free-market capitalism, however, American Corporations are free to become globalist multinational companies should they desire; however, as soon as a corporation transitions from being an American company into a multinational company, it should lose access to American taxpayer benefits and government incentives. American taxpayer money should be focused on helping American companies not multinational companies.

Before politicians and mainstream media try to convince the public that China is the enemy, my suggestion is to first convince American corporations and banks that China is the enemy. As I have already stated both of my former unethical employers (Boeing and Amazon) enjoyed and prioritized doing business with the Chinese government to the point where both of these corporations had a flagrant disregard for America, American citizens, and American moral values.

Freedom is what made America the best nation on earth; and the decline of this freedom is why America will eventually collapse. The globalist American government and the globalist American corporations are working in unison to reduce the constitutional civil liberties that all US citizens are entitled to. Through the deterioration of individual freedoms, this globalist entity will establish more and more control over America and its citizens. Many tactics will be used and have already been used such as:

1) **Fear.** Government and corporations say you need to relinquish your rights and freedoms for your own safety. "Be deathly afraid of Covid."

2) **Comfort.** Government and corporations say you need to relinquish your rights and freedoms, and your lives will be easier and more enjoyable. "Socialism is happiness."

3) **Guilt**. Government and corporations say you need to relinquish your rights and freedoms or you will be branded as outcasts. "Racists are not welcome."

Freedom is not free. Throughout history, American service members have sacrificed their lives for American freedom. However, the patriotism of the US military has also changed. American service members are no longer fighting for the freedoms of US citizens; they are servants to the globalists via the military-industrial complex, they have turned into Government Mercenaries. To both active duty military as well as to veterans,

What American freedoms are you fighting to protect?

Fighting for Freedom

Free speech is under constant attack in America; as this freedom continues to be eroded; the question again is presented to the US military; if you are not fighting to protect basic freedom of speech for all American citizens, then what exactly are you fighting for? The military patriot is the most important citizen in a country. Without military patriots, there is no country, there is no freedom, there is no America. Therefore, specifically to America's military veterans, remember our historic legacy. Beginning in the days of the revolutionary war, West Point, the oldest active US military base in existence, was revered by General Washington as being the "key to the continent." Every time a constitutional freedom in American is restricted, revoked, diluted, altered, abolished, or any other form of transgression, it is up to you, the defenders of American freedom, to stand up to this globalist tyranny and demand liberty. Otherwise, we must be willing to fight and die for this liberty as our military forefathers had to do. It is time for veterans to question their service. Are they serving the American citizens, or are they serving the corporations and government? Any attack on civil liberties is an attack on American citizens. It is time for American veterans to understand that the greatest threat to America and its citizens is not a foreign threat but a domestic one. China is not an ally of America, but it is not an enemy. The government, FBI, and U.S. law enforcement have done more damage to the civil liberties of US citizens than China could ever do.

> **Greater love has no one than this, that he lay down his life for his friends.**
> **—John 15:13**

In 2010, I left the USA to escape the American liberal decay and learn more about leadership in foreign lands, as well as to become a China expert. Despite my departure the American government has continued to illegally spy on me and ruthlessly damage my life. It may be impossible to truly escape the tyrannical grip of the globalist American government—even if one renounces their US citizenship. To those American patriots who wish to remain in America and hold your ground, I salute you and offer you the following advice:

1. **Consider patriotic flight.** We've all heard of the term "white flight" where white people flee urban areas. I recommend you consider patriotic flight or conservative flight and flee liberal blue states and cities to more conservative states and cities. Strength is in numbers, and patriots must surround themselves with like-minded citizens.

2. **Focus on state politics.** As the demographics and diversity in America continue to change toward the detriment of American patriots, sooner or later the goal of winning and leading at the federal level may be out of reach. Therefore, state politics will become the new hotly contested battleground. America's state governors, specifically in the red states, will be thrust to new heights in leadership as American patriots will demand loyalty from their state representatives to put their red state first over the federal government and America as a whole.

3. **Stockpile guns and ammo.** The Second Amendment is without a doubt the most important freedom that a US citizen can exercise because without the Second Amendment all other freedoms can easily be revoked. American patriots must arm themselves and be ready to utilize these arms in the protection of themselves, their families, and their way of life.

4. **Invest in gold and crypto.** The US dollar sooner or later will no longer be the world's reserve currency, and American patriots must be prepared when this happens. Having a secure and independent store of wealth is extremely important. Precious metals and cryptocurrencies are good examples of stores of wealth. Buying land and property, especially self-sufficient farmland is also a strategic purchase.

5. **Be fit to fight.** Without one's health and fitness combat is ineffective. Strive to keep yourself healthy using natural methods. The American government and corporations want to keep the citizens drugged up as a way to both control them

and to also profit off them. Believe in your mind, body, and spirit; have faith.

6. **Push for more dialogue.** As liberal propagandists continue to brainwash Americans into believing diversity is our strength, American patriots already know this to be a lie. American voters must compel their elected officials to begin open and frank conservations about peaceful and piecemeal legal separation of the Union on the basis of freedom of choice.

7. **Form a Western alliance.** The liberal globalist control is not just present in the United States but is now the norm in all Western countries. Canadian patriots, German patriots, Australian patriots, British patriots, Irish patriots are all suffering similar fates. American patriots should reach out to their Western patriot brothers in other countries to form a greater alliance.

8. **Educate yourself.** Remember Bread and Circus—as in Rome so in today's American empire. Stop wasting your money and time on mindless entertainment; instead, get a real-world education. The last NFL Super Bowl I watched was more than fifteen years ago. I do not miss it. The world has so much more to offer and so much more to teach you. Stop the addictions and begin the path to obtain wisdom.

9. **Find God.** Where there is leadership there must be faith. Remember your relationship with God. Every leader must have God in his life. Find him; he is always there, always waiting for you.

10. **Avoid racist propaganda.** American patriots need to stop being scared of being called racist, white supremacist, and Nazi. These are all baseless labels used to undermine the patriotism in America. After living so long in China, I have completely changed my view on racism. Remember that America is the least racist country on earth.

Diversity in scarcity is a strength.
Diversity in abundance is a detriment.

If American patriots are to succeed, then the leadership principle of loyalty must be returned to America. Fidelity is no longer common in marriage, work, family, society, and culture. Infidelity will tear the family, society, and country apart; this is one of the main reasons why Americans are living such lonely lives. They rarely have any true friends who will remain loyal to them through the hard times. Americans are individualistic, and individuals are more vulnerable to tyrannical government and corporation control. The reason why the government does not like militias is like why corporations do not like unions. Loyal and unified groups are harder to control, intimidate, and destroy than disloyal and diversified Individuals.

During my time in the FBI, there was one particular occasion that made me reflect on the principle of loyalty. I was asked to help out another squad, which was conducting a raid on a home. The case agent wanted to execute a search warrant and arrest warrant. It was a counterterrorism (CT) case. The details were given on a need-to-know basis, and I did not ask any questions. During the execution of the warrant, I was to be the front man and breach the door of the home in the early morning hours; that is just what I did. Once inside the home, we quickly scanned for threats and detained all persons inside. After the home was secure and everyone inside was handcuffed, I then took a passive role and provided security. The case agent in charge and the squad began to conduct a thorough search of the entire home. They separated the suspects for interrogations. I was told to guard two of the arrested subjects. I sat the handcuffed pair down on the couch in the living room and conducted another sweep of their bodies for weapons or contraband. The case agent read them their Miranda rights, but they both agreed to talk. I thought it was odd that the two suspects were not separated during the questioning. I stood guard over them as the case agent began his questioning of the pair (a man and a woman). From the onset of the interrogation, it became immediately apparent to me that this couple was in fact a husband and a wife. The case agent of course probably knew this already. It was obvious that they were involved in some type of criminal matter. As the case agent continued his interrogation, he focused mostly on the husband. The questioning lasted for about ten minutes until the case agent ordered the man to be transported to the federal building to be arraigned. After the husband was taken outside, the case agent removed the wife's handcuffs. The case agent thanked the woman for her help as he sat down on the couch beside her. At this time, I was asked to leave as my duty was over. As I left the home; I could still hear the woman and the agent planning their next steps. It was obvious that the woman was an FBI asset who was working against her own husband. As I walked back to my vehicle, I felt something was wrong. As I sat in my vehicle preparing to leave, I pondered at what I had just witnessed: the FBI pushing for a wife to betray her own husband.

The US government has condoned and facilitated the betrayal among family members for the purpose of enforcing the law. This phenomenon is not new. In fact, it is normal protocol for US law enforcement and US intelligence. The January 6 investigations by the FBI was yet another occasion when the FBI pitted family and friends against each other for the purpose of aiding the criminal investigation or gathering intelligence. Legality superseding morality. I never supported this type of disloyalty, and I still do not condone it. Once the government has so much control over the citizens that they will betray their own father and deny God, it then reigns supreme in the land. Anytime there are stories in America of citizens betraying their own family and trusted friends, America should take note as the end is near.

If a country makes more laws, then it will create more criminals.
—Daoist Philosophy

As a former FBI agent who has witnessed the inside culture of the American security apparatus, I can say with absolute confidence that most federal agents will blindly follow the orders of the unethical FBI management. One can be a supporter of US law enforcement and at the same time have no tolerance for the decline of individual freedoms and civil liberties. We must always remind law enforcement that they work at the behest of the American public; they are sworn to serve and protect US citizens.

The globalist government and globalist corporations want to replace strong American men; they view us as a threat. Big government and big corporations want to transform America into a socialist state, where instead of men being responsible for providing for and protecting the women and children, government and corporations will do the job. As a result, American men will become more and more marginalized. Throughout history women and children have relied upon their men for protection, but now the globalist government does the protecting. It has replaced men by making them weak and subordinate. Throughout history women and children have relied on the men to provide for them, but now globalist corporations dominate the economy. They strive to prevent men from running their own businesses and becoming financially independent.

The destruction of America begins and ends with the destruction of American men. Independent, brave, resilient, strong, loyal, rebellious, responsible, tough, proud are the qualities of the American patriot. These are the men who are willing to fight for **Faith, Family,** and **Freedom.**

When I lived in China I was surprised at how many Chinese movies and television shows highlight the glory of China's history. The Chinese are very proud of their history and of their forefathers. What a contrast to America's attitude regarding our Founding Fathers and the liberal contempt for these so-called racist white men. If you are a proud American, then you should be proud of our Founding Fathers. If you believe America is a great country, then you should believe our Founding Fathers were great men.

It all begins with our voice. Forced segregation is immoral and illegal; however, forced integration is also immoral and illegal. Forced integration has its roots in communism; it also leads to conflict and disharmony. It is time for American citizens to have the freedom to self-regulate their own private lives, communities, and affairs. They should have free will and be able to choose who they will allow to participate within their own private living sphere. American citizens must be given the right and freedom to take back their private communities and be able to freely choose who they desire to live amongst, which will be most likely be like-minded people. Diversity is destroying America; and freedom is the answer to the problem.

**All is foreseen, and freedom of choice is
granted.**
—Ethics of the Fathers 3:15

My own government has designated me as an enemy of the state with no evidence of wrongdoing relating to national security. Instead, the FBI has thus focused their investigation on my conversative political views as justification for their unconstitutional spy campaign against me. Despite my patriotic service to America, my own government has chosen to discard my constitutional rights as a US citizen and treat me like a national security threat. As the American liberal globalist government welcomes foreigners, immigrants, and refugees into the country, I am not welcome to my home country, the same country I have served as a US Army officer. The American government has arbitrarily garnished my overseas wages as payment for tax revenue; therefore, my tax money is welcome back in America, however I myself am not. When I visited America, I was detained, interrogated, searched, humiliated, surveilled, deceived, and assaulted by my very own government to which our tax-money supports. Due to my conservative political views, the government has illegally and immorally been spying on me and so many other innocent Americans for years. Their spy campaign against me has included collaboration with foreign governments and thus has put my life in danger and destroyed my livelihood. What is happening to me has also occurred and is occurring to so many other unwitting innocent US citizens. Almost all Americans will never come to know about the government's spy operations against them. It is protected under the guise of national security.

As the situation in America becomes more desperate, more Americans will also be designated as enemies of the state. When American military veterans are deemed threats to the country, then the end of America is near. Without the patriotic loyalty of military veterans to support the government, then the government itself will be deemed as a tyrannical threat by the American public.

The American globalist corporations work hand and hand with the globalist government, as their revenue streams have become more intimately derived from taxpayer money. In the end, these globalist corporations and globalist government will work together to control and dominate the American people. These corporations are not loyal to the American people. They are happy to propagate the idea that China is the enemy, yet at the same time eagerly partner with China on business deals. Through crony corporate capitalism, America has already been bought and sold, and the American taxpayer is paying the ultimate price. Through the liberal globalist brainwashing that diversity is our strength, the American family has been destroyed, the American faith has been destroyed, and now American freedoms are being destroyed. Everything that our great ancestors died for is now being pushed closer to extinction. If the Founding Fathers were alive to witness today's America, how would they evaluate the liberal and globalist takeover of the country? How would they evaluate the hatred targeted against strong Christian heterosexual white men? How would they evaluate the tyrannical government and corporations? More important, how would they evaluate those brave patriots who are now willing to rebel against this tyranny?

American patriots, we have the blood of rebel leadership running in our veins. Through their bravery, our forefathers won freedom and independence from the tyrannical British empire. Bravery will once

again be needed to win freedom and independence from today's
tyrannical American empire. If there is no freedom, then there is no
America. As the American system continues to deteriorate, more and
more freedoms will be denied to the citizens. The tyrannical globalist
control over America will continue until the breaking point is reached.
The strongest a man can ever be is with his faith in God; it is time to
return to faith. Put your faith in God and trust him to guide you
through the darkness of the disaster that will befall America. Never
forget what we are fighting for: **Faith, Family,** and **Freedom.**

Like all empires, sooner or later America will also come to an end.
There was a time when America was truly the beaming light of freedom
and hope throughout the world; however, now the so-called
diplomatic rules-based system that America touts is in fact a globalist
system where America sets the global rules and therefore rules over
everyone. Through greed and globalism, the America government and
corporations are now seen both domestically and abroad as a force of
domination as opposed to freedom. American corporations' global
pursuit for profits have left them with as little ethical concerns for their
foreign partners—as they have for their very own American citizens.
More and more countries are desiring a world where America is no
longer the supreme "boss." Even American citizens have grown tired
and angry with the government's constant expansion of powers and
control over the civil liberties of the citizens in the constant pursuit to
be the world's policeman. The American government and American
corporations continue to strip away the rights and freedoms of US
citizens: the right to free speech, the right to privacy, the right to raise
your children, the right to be a strong man, the right to a clean
environment, the right to freedom of association, the right to tax
money accountability, the right to bear arms, the right to have

sovereignty over your own body, the right to be proud of your history, the right to be proud of your race, the right to put God before all else, the right to live a free life. At the same time, US citizens are told that our deadliest enemies are outside of America. Our government constantly points to foreign countries and foreign actors as the primary threat to the American way of life. Remember the ridiculous war on terror and the supposed evil Taliban? How has the war in Afghanistan improved the lives of ordinary American citizens? This is the same unethical pattern of propaganda being targeted at China. The biggest threat to the freedoms of US citizens is not found overseas in foreign lands; the biggest threat is right here in America. The globalist government and globalist corporations will continue to push their rule over American citizens, thus denying them of life, liberty, and the pursuit of happiness. To the American patriots, may God grant us strength, and may God ultimately cast blind judgement upon America. Freedom is not free; from our fathers to our sons, let the destiny of the American man unravel yet again through the struggle and sacrifice to which fear and danger await us. This is the time for warrior leadership.

To the Patriots: Thank you for joining me on this personal leadership journey, what has happened to me at the hands of the tyrannical government and globalist corporations can so easily happen to you, this betrayal is our rally point. I hope we may meet each other one day on the high ground. As the dragons and beasts assemble in the valley below, bringing with them the fear of death. May we stand firm and stand together, like Knights in combat. Our time on earth will run its course, but our legacy like our forefathers, will live on. Our fate lies in the hands of God, so let us Grips Hands and prepare for battle.

> **When you have no choice,**
> **mobilize the spirit of courage.**
> **—Jewish Proverb**

FAITH – FAMILY – FREEDOM

About the Author

David Baumblatt is a former FBI agent and US Army officer who was born and raised in New York by a Jewish father and German mother. Convinced of an impending collapse of the American society due to the increasing negative influence and collusion of globalist corporations and globalist government, David left America in 2010 and moved to China where he has lived for over ten years. The founder and CEO of Terebinth Leadership Advisory, David's consulting work focuses on three strategic leadership challenges: (1) Change Leadership, (2) China Leadership, and (3) Crisis Leadership.

His education includes:

- Harvard University: Master Public Administration
- IMD Switzerland: Master Business Administration
- University of San Francisco: Master Chinese Studies
- University of Oklahoma: Master Human Relations
- US Military Academy (West Point): Bachelor of Science
- Marion Military Institute: Associate of Arts

Designated a national security threat and unconstitutionally spied on, David is no longer welcome to return to America due to the corrupt US government's immoral and illegal retaliation against him. David is based in Hong Kong and enjoys studying the spiritual teachings of both Judaism and Daoism. His political ideology centers upon Faith, Family, and Freedom. He is fluent in Mandarin Chinese and German. His website is www.terebinth.info.

Notes

Acknowledgments

1 康达律师事务所 Kāng dá lǜshī shìwù suǒ Kangda Law Firm is a large full-service law firm headquartered in Beijing, China. It was founded in 1988 and is among the first private partnership law firms approved by the Ministry of Justice of China. The firm has won many honors, including "National Outstanding Law Firm" and "Beijing Outstanding Law Firm" several times.

2 Lawyer Xushuo 许硕: www.kangdalawyers.com/news/2230.html.

Chapter 1: New York Upbringing

1 咏春 – Yǒng chūn Chinese Martial Arts focused on close-quarters hand-to-hand combat.

2 熊朝忠 – xióng cháozhōng The first Chinese Boxer to ever win a boxing world title; WBC mini-flyweight title from 2012 to 2014.

Chapter 2: Real World Leadership

1 阴阳 yīnyáng Yin and yang is a Chinese philosophical concept that describes opposite but interconnected forces. In Daoist metaphysics, distinctions between good and bad, along with other dichotomous moral judgments, are perceptual, not real; so, the duality of yin and yang is an indivisible whole.

2 危机 wéijī In the Chinese language, the word "crisis" is composed of two characters, one representing danger and the other, opportunity.

Chapter 5: Patriotism

1 人民币 rénmínbì The People's Currency; abbreviation: RMB is the official currency of the People's Republic of China.

2 Hall of Heroes: American Jewish Recipients of the Medal of Honor, https://nmajmh.org/exhibitions/permanent-exhibitions/hall-of-heroes/.

Chapter 6: Fake Feminism

[1] 剩女 Shèngnǚ Leftover women is a derogatory term popularized by the All-China Women's Federation that classifies women who remain unmarried in their late twenties and beyond. Most prominently used in China, the term has also been used colloquially to refer to women in India, North America, Europe, and other parts of Asia. The term compares unmarried women to leftover food and has gone on to become widely used in the mainstream media and has been the subject of several television series, magazine and newspaper articles, and book publications, focusing on the negative connotations and positive reclamation of the term.

Chapter 8: Defund the Police

[1] 成都 chéngdū A sub-provincial city which serves as the capital of the Chinese province of Sichuan. 四川 sìchuān is a province in Southwest China with a population of 83 million.

Chapter 10: China Is the Not the Enemy

[1] 中医 zhōngyī Traditional Chinese Medicine is an ancient system of traditional medicine developed in China over thousands of years.

[2] 北京烤鸭 běijīng kǎoyā Peking duck is a dish from Beijing that has been prepared since the Imperial era.

[3] 孙武 sūnwǔ Famous Chinese military strategist, known as "the master of a hundred generations of military strategists" and "the originator of Oriental strategics". Author of the book: Sun Tzu's Art of War.

[4] 孙子兵法 sūnzi bīngfǎ *The Art of War* is an ancient Chinese military treatise dating from the fifth century BC. It is the most influential strategy text in East Asian warfare and has influenced both East Asian and Western military theory and thinking and has found a variety of applications in a myriad of competitive non-military endeavors across the modern world including espionage, culture, politics, business, and sports.

[5] 新疆 xīnjiāng Xinjiang is an autonomous region located in the northwest China. It spans over 620,000 square miles and has about 25 million inhabitants.

[6] 维吾尔族 Wéiwú'ěr zú Uyghur is a Turkic-speaking people living in the interior of Eurasia, mainly using Uyghur, which belongs to the Turkic language and is based on the Persian Arabic alphabet Old Uyghur script. The majority of Uyghurs are Sunni in Islam.

Chapter 11: Corporate Capitalism

1 舟山 Zhōushān Zhoushan is an urbanized archipelago with the administrative status of a prefecture level city in the eastern Chinese province of Zhejiang.

2 "Boeing to Pay $200 Million to Settle SEC Charges that it Misled Investors about the 737 MAX," US Securities and Exchange Commission Press Release, September 22, 2022, https://www.sec.gov/news/press-release/2022-170.

3 "How we act" Boeing *Our Values* web page, https://www.boeing.com/principles/values.page.

4 Goldman, Jonathan C | Goldman & Ehrlich, https://www.goldmanehrlich.com/attorney/goldman-jonathan-c/.

5 Baum v. Boeing (China) Co., No. 17 C 7647 (US N.D. Ill. Eastern Div., 2020).

6 United States District Court, ND of Illinois, Eastern Division, "Court Information Release," August 4, 2020, https://www.ilnd.uscourts.gov/_assets/_news/Diversity_Committee_PressRelease_FINAL.pdf.

7 Women & Law, New York University Law Review, Febrary 2020, https://www.nyulawreview.org/wp-content/uploads/2020/02/Women-Law-Full-PDF.pdf.

8 U.S. Equal Employment Opportunity Commission, "Retaliation," https://www.eeoc.gov/privacy-policy-us-equal-employment-opportunity-commission-web-site-and-mobile-app.

Chapter 12: Nationalism Is Unity

1 习近平 Xíjìnpíng General Secretary of the Chinese Communist Party.

2 汉族 Hànzú The Han Chinese are an East Asian ethic group native to China. They are the world´s largest ethnic group, making up about 18% of the global population. Originating from Northern China, the Han Chinese trace their ancestry to the Huaxia, a confederation of agricultural tribes that lived along the Yellow River.

3 华侨 Huáqiáo Overseas Chinese refers to people of Chinese birth or ethnicity who reside outside Mainland China, Hong Kong, Macau, and Taiwan.

4 道教 – dàojiào Daoism is the native religion of China, its ideas originated from the Yellow Emperor with a significant attention to the unity of man and nature.

5 "What are the racial proportions among Singapore citizens?" Singapore Government portal, 10 Dec 2019, https://www.gov.sg/article/what-are-the-racial-proportions-among-singapore-citizens.

Chapter 13: European Replacement

[1] 少数民族 Shǎoshù mínzú Ethnic minorities in China are the non-Han Chinese population in the People's Republic of China. China officially recognizes 55 ethnic minority groups within China in addition to the Han majority.

[2] 昆明 Kūnmíng Kunming is the capital and largest city of Yunnan province, China.

[3] 云南 Yúnnán Yunnan is a landlocked province in the southwest of the People's Republic of China. The province spans approximately 152,000 square miles and has a population of 48.3 million (as of 2018).

[4] 乌鲁木齐 Wūlǔmùqí Ürümqi is the capital of the Xinjiang Uyghur Autonomous Region in the far northwest of the People's Republic of China.

[5] 简体字 Jiǎntǐzì Simplified Chinese characters are one type of standard Chinese character sets. Along with traditional Chinese characters, they are one of the two standard character sets of the contemporary Chinese written language. The government of the People's Republic of China in mainland China has promoted them for use in printing since the 1950s and 1960s to encourage literacy. They are officially used in the People's Republic of China, Malaysia, and Singapore, while traditional Chinese characters remain in common use in Hong Kong, Macau, Taiwan and Japan, as well as South Korea to a certain extent.

[6] 身份证 Shēnfèn zhèng Chinese Resident Identity Card which is very much comparable to a driver's license. On it, your picture, your name, your gender, ethnic group, date of birth, address, and ID number are present. Now, chips have been added and embedded within the cards that can be scanned as well.